STAY ALERT
STAY ALIVE

The NeighborHOOD Individual Protective Guide

Kevin Andre White

AMERICAN SOCIETY FOR INDUSTRIAL SECURITY (ASIS)
CERTIFIED PROTECTION PROFESSIONAL (CPP) #14280

authorHOUSE®

AuthorHouse™
1663 Liberty Drive
Bloomington, IN 47403
www.authorhouse.com
Phone: 1-800-839-8640

Published by AuthorHouse 3/22/2012

ISBN: 978-1-4343-2211-1 (sc)
ISBN: 978-1-4343-2213-5 (e)

GENERAL KNOWLEDGE

This security awareness checklist booklet provides recommended individual protective steps primarily for people who live or work in high crime or poverty stricken areas. One should remember that this information can be applied anywhere in the United States and/or World!

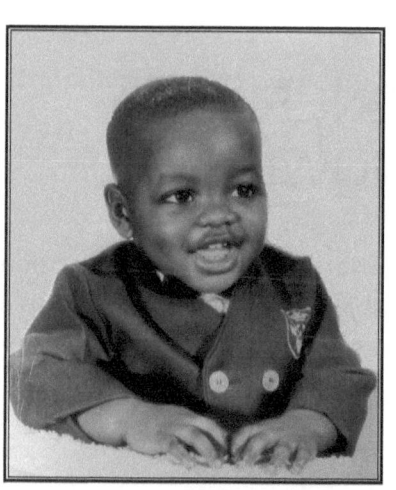

CONTENTS

FOREWORD

As an African American who spent the early years of my life growing up as a minority in a low income, high crime community, I find it extremely important to impart some of the individual protective knowledge tips I have acquired since October 8, 1962 and during my 30 year career working as a United States Air Force (USAF) Security Policeman in effort to help protect good people from criminals. Hopefully the knowledge and experience I gained working as a Defense Threat Reduction Agency (DTRA) Physical Protection System Project Manager, Headquarters Air Force Special Operations Command Chief of Force Protection (i.e., chief physical security, anti-terrorism, police operations, etc), Police Shift Sergeant, Nuclear Security Alarm Monitor, Security Force Dispatcher, Security Police Patrolman, and Access Controller is communicated in such a way that you can readily apply recommended fundamentals that should help you prevent becoming a victim of criminal incidents. Additionally, the knowledge I have gained as an American Military University (AMU) Homeland Security Masters graduate, an AMU Criminal Justice Bachelor's graduate, and an USAF Community College Security Administration Associates graduate will be used to thoroughly prepare you! The intent of this checklist booklet is to get YOU, the individual citizen, thinking in the right direction as you maneuver in a high crime or poverty-stricken community located anywhere in the world. People should keep in mind that just because they do not reside in one of these areas, does not mean criminal acts will not occur. Therefore, this individual protective guide is meant to be a "pocket sized booklet" designed to be easily carried on your person where it is readily available for use. There is nothing extremely special or difficult about the security awareness checklists provided. They are simply created to aid in the precautions you take daily to ensure your personal safety. Each checklist was created as a stand-alone guide. Therefore information contained in one checklist may be contained in another.

INTRODUCTION

This booklet comes at a time when society seems to be most vulnerable, where large groups of young Americans are not effectively groomed for professional success, when decent policemen hired to protect society are too few, and when some police personnel and politicians have become participants in criminal activities most citizens wish to evade. Our personal safety is paramount! No longer can we walk the streets in peace, routinely greeting people in a pleasant manner and expecting the same behavior in return. The average person must be aware of people attempting to steal their belongings, molest or rape them, physically assault them, or even murder them for one of numerous reasons that have become apparent in society today. A few specific threats people must be aware of in modern times is the ever growing criminal element threat; the ever growing domestic and especially foreign terrorist threat that endangers Americans worldwide; and the long standing anti-minority threat posed towards African, Arab, Asian, Hispanic, Jewish, Native Americans and bi-racial citizens, to include European Americans who are supportive of these cultures. This ideology is presented by some Americans who live and breathe the ideals of "Supremacy." In most cases this ideology leads to physical assault, murder, forced minority subordination, minority disenfranchisement, unjust imprisonment, and ultimately, a goal of minority elimination.

Having communicated this direct message, an understanding person must realize the above statement does not refer to the vast majority of good, descent, "God Fearing" Americans or foreigners, but only to the ever enlarging criminal and terrorist organizations which may impose harm upon a nation's citizens and/or tourist due to hate, revenge and/or economic greed.

Please remember the basic goal of this individual protective guide is for people to become more aware of evils that confront us in society today, and take the precautions to better protect our families. To put it simply, failure to take the appropriate protective actions may lead to **YOU** or someone you love becoming the next victim Americans or foreigners hear about on the six o'clock news, or view some years later at a holocaust museum!

All I ask is that you make a conscientious effort to protect yourself, family, friends, and other love ones! If distinguished people like Martin Luther King and countless other Americans had access to this protective guidance, then perhaps they would be alive today! The statistics indicated below communicated by the Department of Justice (DOJ), Federal Bureau of Investigation (FBI) on their CRIME CLOCK 2009 web page should help motivate you!

CRIME CLOCK 2009: The frequency of various Crimes as reported by the DOJ & FBI by minutes and second they occur.

Violent Crime	**23.9 seconds**
One Murder every	35.4 minutes
One Forcible Rape every	6 minutes
One Robbery every	1.3 minutes
One Aggravated Assault every	31.9 seconds
Property Crimes	**3.4 seconds**
One Burglary every	14.3 seconds
One Larceny-theft every	5 seconds
One Motor Vehicle Theft every	39.7 seconds

Please take this information to heart and do not become a victim! Furthermore, please recognize this document is not written for entertainment value, but as a serious pamphlet designed to provide basic individual protective techniques. This checklist booklet is not intended to replace any technique or practice you have already implemented to ensure your personnel protection. It is by no means all-inclusive, but is primarily meant to provide guidance that will enhance your ability to protect yourself and love ones.

Kevin A. White
Author

CHECKLIST 1
Causation of Crime Checklist

Before we progress into the following checklist which will provide general guidance on individual protection steps, I believe we must gain a basic understanding about the causation of crime. Well, many people sometimes wonder why humans steal, murder, commit terrorist acts and/or commit other hideous crimes/evil acts; but **Criminologist Donald Cressey** points out in Paul Purpura's book called "Security and Loss Prevention" [2002] that there are three key elements which offer insight into the cause of crime and labeled this concept *"The Crime Triangle"* as listed/defined below:

The Crime Triangle:

▶ **Motivation (or Need Satisfaction):** e.g., desire for power, jobs, land, money, merchandise, jewels, love interest, religious ideological goals, etc.

▶ **Opportunity:** e.g., being in the vicinity to carry out your crime with a low possibility of being observed, stopped, or caught; or having political power to create unjust laws that put you in a powerful position to carry out evil atrocities; or you simply have the weaponry in hand to force people to follow your direction; or you have a key position in the system (e.g., charismatic political or religious leader, etc) which gives you the opportunity to safely conduct and/or motivate evil acts without retaliation; or you have the power to mentally control people with low self-esteem like prisoners, some young humans, people in need of basic survival resources, or under-educated humans, etc.

▶ **Rationalization:** e.g., *your mental excuse to justify evil acts* via belief that God/Jehovah/Allah/Buddha/Kali/ etc made you commit some criminal act as thoroughly outlined by Bruce Hoffman, in his book titled, "Inside Terrorism [1998]"; or, belief that some society is greedy and evil, and the people must correct them; or I was created to be superior; or they were not using it correctly anyway; or finders keepers—losers weepers concept; or survival of the fittest human concept (instead of human brotherhood concept); or they are rich and it will not hurt them financially; or it is my body and I can do what I want with it; and/or personal belief that **human rule or law** does not make sense, so the "catch-me-if-you-can" concept is rationalized/executed, etc.

However, I must communicate that people should know the **Crime Triangle** can be reversed for good purposes where it can be seen as the **Heavenly Triangle** (see example below):

The Heavenly Triangle:

▶ **Motivation/Need:** to help others via charity, etc.

▶ **Opportunity:** the person has the monetary assets to accomplish the task.

▶ **Rationalization:** God, Jehovah, Allah, Buddha, etc would want people to do well unto others and/or a personal belief in helping uplift the human race is a positive virtue!

* See how these three components can also be used for good actions?

This is good information for regular citizens, security managers and law enforcement officers to know in effort to better understand the root causes of criminal activity. Yet, as you will find in criminal justice criminology studies, scientist have communicated several causes for crime to include poverty and the inhalation of poisonous chemicals that may decrease effective brain operations, which are critical if humans are to non-violently/honestly provide for themselves.

SPECIAL NOTE: Each checklist was created as a stand-alone guide. Therefore information contained in one checklist may be contained in another.

CHECKLIST 2
Threat Awareness Checklist

Please coordinate with the following centers indicated below to obtain current criminal knowledge that may assist you in protecting yourself and family. Although you may find it strange to talk with some of the authorities listed below, they will be even more shocked you asked the question! Just remember to ask questions concerning your home of residence or areas you plan to visit. Be specific by asking what types of crimes have taken place in the area, and if there are any criminal gangs, child molesters, and/or hate groups present. Next, take precautions accordingly.

Actions/Tips:

► Solicit support from local Police Department.

► Solicit support from local FBI Office.

► Read the newspaper or online news programs daily. It could provide warning of a criminal act.

► Ask residents about the safety of the neighborhood.

► If traveling overseas, check the Department of State Foreign Travel Advisory for information on specific countries.

  ▷ Always solicit support from local U.S. Embassy and maintain contact once you arrive. You will want to contact the Embassy's Regional Security Office (RSO) for support.

  ▷ If you are able to communicate, solicit support

from local Host Nation Police Officials (call ahead if you must).

▷ Follow all safety precautions provided by U.S. Embassy Officials.

► Ensure you brief your family members or traveling party on all information you have received.

► In addition, routinely brief and update police and Embassy officials on threats you have encountered. This information will aid in protecting others.

SPECIAL NOTE: *Each checklist was created as a stand-alone guide. Therefore information contained in one checklist may be contained in another.*

CHECKLIST 3
Individual Protective Steps Checklist

The time is now to take your personal security more seriously than you ever have in the past. Your life could depend on it. Use this checklist to evaluate your personal protection preparedness.

Actions/Tips:

► Have you become aware of the growing danger of living in just about any American community?

► Do you read a local newspaper or online news program at least every other day (could inform you of local or national criminal activity)?

► Do you communicate positively with local police (a good police relationship is beneficial—helps them see you as a positive person in the community)?

► Do you watch the local news on television daily (could inform of local criminal activity)?

► Do you feel you can protect yourself (e.g., taking actions to make yourself a harder, more difficult target)?

► Have you checked to see if local laws authorize the use of a concealed handgun, mace, or other protective weapons (some states license these weapons)?

► Do you conduct a simple background investigation on medical doctors you visit (some have extreme rightwing views—you could become a victim of the evil scientist, which has taken place in human society countless times!)?

▶ Do you conduct a thorough investigation on people or organizations that provide your child care service—criminals could be employed?

▶ Do you check with local police to determine if convicted child molesters or rapist reside in your community?

▶ Do you select your friends and associates wisely (looking for positive, trustworthy, good people)?

▶ Do you take steps not to reside or associate with characters that may put you into a harmful situation (e.g., known drug dealers, illegal drug users, hate groups, or other criminal personalities)?

▶ Do you participate in neighborhood watch programs?

▶ Do you communicate with neighbors to determine local threats (i.e., hate groups, gangs, or other criminal threats) and high crime areas?

▶ Do you read magazines or review Internet web pages to gain personal protection information?

▶ Have you conducted research to determine if there is a high criminal threat or terrorist threat to your place of residence?

▶ Can you obtain adequate criminal threat information from local law enforcement authorities?

▶ Do you routinely vary your route and mode of transportation?

▶ Do you secure your vehicle when not in use?

▶ If a terrorist and/or hate group threat is present, do you search your car/vehicle prior to use?

▶ Does your place of residence offer you protection from criminals (i.e., alarm systems, environmental friendly protective window devices, or security guards services, etc.)?

▶ Does your lodging location provide protection from terrorist or criminal acts?

▶ Does your place of work provide protection from terrorist acts (i.e., building security, alarm systems, or hardened facilities)?

▶ Does your employer place emphasis on protection of assigned employees/personnel?

▶ Is a communication system in place at your work center (or home) to warn employees and/or family members of an imminent or actual terrorist/criminal attack (e.g., public address system or computer warning program in which computer specialist can transmit alarm messages to all assigned facility computers—warning should automatically appear on monitor)?

▶ Could you render CPR or first-aid/buddy care following a terrorist or violent criminal attack?

▶ Do you effectively communicate local individual protective steps with your family members or traveling party?

▶ Do you take a friend or pet (dog) with you when walking through the neighborhood?

▶ If out on the town and unarmed, do you travel in groups of two or larger (e.g., This technique will make you a harder target for criminals to engage. It is much easier to assault a lone individual)?

▶ If you are promiscuous, do you practice safe sexual contact (e.g., Today, sexually transmitted diseases like the many viruses that cause AIDS are among the leading causes of death among minorities 18-44 years old, and is now considered a worldwide plague)?

▶ Have you established a will in case of your sudden death? If you are in the military, have you established a will or a power of attorney via your legal office? **NOTE:** James Brown, the God Father of Soul failed to update his will; and upon his death it caused many problems for his acting spouse and their baby son.

▶ Have you developed a lecture or power point briefing to routinely brief your children (at least bi-monthly) on how to safely and successfully maneuver in American life!

▶ This list can go on and on, but I think I covered solid ground!

SPECIAL NOTE: Each checklist was created as a stand-alone guide. Therefore information contained in one checklist may be contained in another.

CHECKLIST 4
Avoiding Childhood Dangers Checklist

Many people will see the picture on the front cover of this book and say, **"What a happy little boy!"** Well, in life all humans go through ups and downs, regardless of their economic strata in America, and I definitely had my share. You see, I was my mother's first born child and she became impregnated with me at the early age of 19 where her life skills were limited. Moreover, if it were not for the Church she would have received even less mentoring as she attempted to navigate through this thing called "LIFE". As a result of her lack of effective nurturing on how to take advantage of opportunity (which was definitely not equivalent for African Americans of the 1950's/1960's era as it is in the 21st Century) she did not develop the essential communication skills required to impart critical protection or security knowledge to me. Therefore, I grew up in a society where people cared little about African American boys to include others labeled black who walked the same street. Yet, I realized (for some unknown reason) I had to take specific steps to enhance my personal safety in order to survive without being assaulted each day—perhaps this intuition was FEAR (?). So, what were these steps that helped me maneuver through a sometimes violent America? Well, I have listed these protective steps below in hopes informed Americans benchmark and communicate them to their family and/or friends in a manner that they can understand and effectively protect themselves.

Actions/Tips:

▶ Observe your surrounding—a lot can be learned by just watching people interact with others. In doing this, I learned as a child that people (regardless of culture/race) fall within four general categories (i.e., bad, mediocre, good, or great people). To be honest, I learned the majority of people appeared to be bad or mediocre; therefore, I avoided them whenever possible, and I still do today in effort to reduce all facets of human negativity.

▶ It must be stated the young people have a high desire to belong to the in-crowd (i.e., that socially accepted group); therefore, if your child is considered an outsider (i.e., a nerd, an introvert, or egotistical, etc) they may be selected by members of the in-crowd to harass. Normally this harassment will not come from just the bully community, but most often from people trying to make a name for themselves. Therefore, knowledgeable parents must relate this to their children and attempt to properly clothe and mentor them in order to reduce negative tension they fully know will come otherwise.

▶ Realize now parents must dress their children to fit into the environment they reside. You only need analyze society to figure out what is appropriate and/or selected by the masses. People who dress outside of the norm are normally harassed because they are perceived as being ignorant or a nerd. **NOTE:** Children should take the "middle-road" so-to-speak with clothing dress styles, because they must be accepted by their peers and they must also appear acceptable to the society at large. For instance, urban dress styles taken to the extreme may be misjudged by authorities; thus, bringing negativity into lives. Remember that celebrities are predominately millionaires and do not have to buy into the norms of society; therefore, youngsters will see plenty of celebrities that may dress inappropriately in clothes and hair styles; yet, wise people will realize this and take appropriate actions in their personal lives.

► Children must be taught, if they cannot already perceive what a bad person is, and they must avoid bad people whenever possible. As a child, when I saw known bullies coming down the street, I went the other way. This was particularly important since I was the oldest child and did not have an older sibling to protect me.

► Parents must teach their children how to defend themselves. Although many parents do not want their children to fight, and especially in school, sometimes a child will have to defend themselves or be perceived by an immature group of young people as a weak human that will not defend themselves. And if a child is perceived as weak many people will attempt to gain respect of the in-crowd by harassing the weak human. As a military dependent, whenever I moved to a new American community I was always challenged by some person who was normally not even the community bully, but some person trying to make a name for themselves since they saw me as being a vulnerable loner. Therefore, over time I realized the best way to deal with such humans is to immediately respond to their aggression with aggression. Regardless if I won the encounter or not, the message communicated was that this young man will stand his ground; therefore, all it took was one violent altercation and my life was pleasant from that point on. Now, this worked for me in the 1970's when society was not as violent as society has become in the 21ˢᵗ Century. Yet, regardless of time period, a person must stand up for their rights or lose them. This is one reason **Patrick Henry** proclaimed, **"Give me liberty or give me death!"** And yes, after 9/11 America did not turn the other cheek as communicated by Jesus Christ, but instead took steps to return aggression with aggression!

► Additionally, one way young people can become a member of the in-crowd and avoid persecution is to participate in sports. Generally speaking people enjoy group interaction and especially when it comes to sports. Therefore if your child is nurtured from early childhood about sports participation then normally they will grow up descent athletes and not only be accepted by the in-crowd but are sought out. The same thing applies to children who sing and/or play instruments.

► Furthermore, instruct your kids not to participate in jokes made to put people down. Some people can take a joke, but many people cannot, and this normally leads to revengeful violence. If your child is the recipient of jokes, it is best they handle the jokes in two ways: 1) Either laugh with the crowd and respond by saying something like, "*Yes, my Mother says the same thing.*" Comments like this may deflate the comedian's effort to get laughs and causes them to move toward someone else because the victim is not getting angry—thus, the intended victim becomes no real fun; or 2) Observe the comedian and respond with something more funny (yet not hurtful) about him/her making others laugh; thereby, causing the comedian to retreat. **NOTE:** Fighting because some comedian attacks a person with negative jokes is not recommended or smart! People must wisely deal with comedians to prevent violent responses.

▶ Although our modern society is bombarded by negative music that praises illegal drug use, realize that your children must be educated to stay away from illegal drugs or fall victim to what I call the **"AMERICAN RAT TRAP."**

▶ Strive to educate your family and friend on this thing called the **"AMERICAN RAT TRAP"**. However, the average person may say, "What is the **"AMERICAN RAT TRAP?"** Well, normally when RATS approach a RAT TRAP in pursuit of the CHEESE, they seem to understand the trap could endanger their lives; therefore, they do not just blindly walk into the trap; but instead, patiently attempt to figure out how to negotiate the obstacle and obtain the prize (i.e., the CHEESE). Sometimes the RAT is successful, and most often they are not—they are caught by the RAT TRAP and suffer the consequences. Now, when you apply this scenario to humans the **"CHEESE"** is substituted with **"DESIRE"**. But the desire could be many things like: *using illegal drugs, stealing, assaulting humans, participating in unprotected promiscuous sexual activities, hanging out with criminal elements (e.g., hate groups or criminal gangs/mafias, child moles-*

tation, or infidelity, etc). The thing to remember here is that the majority of humans realize participating in the activities outlined above are wrong, but they do so anyway due to their uncontrolled pursuit of elements they **"DESIRE"**. But just like the majority of RATS are overcome by the RAT TRAP, many humans suffer the same defeats in pursuit of their **"DESIRES."** The end result is they fall for the human **"AMERICAN RAT TRAP"** and suffer the consequences by being shamed, imprisoned (i.e., become modern slaves) and/or are murdered, etc. So, there you have it—the **"AMERICAN RAT TRAP"** that all wise humans, regardless of age must understand and avoid!

▶ **NOTE 1:** Failure to implement these recommended educational tips to protect yourself and youth may lead to a very bad situation as unfortunately communicated by Stars & Stripes in one of their early 2007 newspaper articles (see paraphrased article below):

▷ **STARS & STRIPES PARAPHRASED ARTICLE:** A 14-year old boy chased down a 15-year old boy and shot him in the face at the entrance to a hospital's emergency room, where the victim immediately sought treatment, said authorities. The suspect was tackled by a hospital security guard and placed in handcuffs. The victim was treated at the hospital and then flown by helicopter to Columbus Children's Hospital, where he was in critical condition. **End of Another Atrocious Story!**

▶ **NOTE 2:** If a person decides to bring a child into

this world, they must have a plan to legally provide for their basic human needs (i.e., nourishment/clothing—survival, safety/security, and belonging needs, etc). If not, the DESIRE for a child to obtain these basic human needs may result in illegal acts that may lead to juvenile criminal records, incarceration and/or death. And if all adults are honest, the true blame falls on the PARENT! Therefore, any decision to bring children into the world must be critically thought out, and operational plans developed to productively raise the child. The creation of children must be taken seriously, and having sex is the way healthy humans produce children. Therefore, if humans wants to play with sex for entertainment value, they must take all precautions to prevent having children. Because if they do not, and a child is brought into the world, they must effectively provide for their newborn or suffer the consequences which will come for CERTAIN!

SPECIAL NOTE: *Each checklist was created as a stand-alone guide. Therefore information contained in one checklist may be contained in another.*

CHECKLIST 5
Selecting Friends or Associates Checklist

Some people find it great to be associated with large numbers of people, but as most of us have experienced, this can bring severe grief along with the pleasure of friendship. If having numerous associates is important to you, please ensure these people do not intentionally or accidentally bring harm to you or your family. Use this checklist to help in your selection of friends and associates.

Actions/Tips:

▶ Surround yourself with positive, law-abiding people.

▶ Do not associate with people who tend to live on the edge and take chances that could land them in jail – you could be going right along with them.

▶ Do not associate with people who do illegal drugs. Regardless of what people try to say, drugs are illegal and always causes damage to the body and reputation (i.e., Can Bring Shame to the Entire Family).

▶ Do not participate in gossip conversations generated by your current friends. This could lead to fights that can endanger your personal safety or safety of a loved one.

▶ Strive to select friends who are spiritually connected to some angelic creator (i.e., God, Allah, or Jehovah, Buddha, etc). Chances are—they may have a conscious and want to do good. Yet, realize, some non-believers are <u>extraordinary</u> people.

▶ Unless you know the person closely; <u>consider</u> keeping your distance or stay completely away from people that do not believe in any form of spiritual righteousness. This should be done, because some non-believers may not have a conscious and can turn on you in a violent manner at any given time. *However, do not be brainwashed, since people who proclaim to be spiritually righteous have hurt others since the beginning of time.*

▶ Find friendship in people who are constantly demonstrating their desire to help others.

▶ Find friendship in people who generally have a love for good behavior, and steer away from people who perpetrate evil and/or injustice on others.

▶ Do not let the statue of anyone determine if you should trust them as a friend. Politicians, judges, ministers, teachers, police, and supervisors have historically, and in modern times—harmed citizens; therefore, keep your eyes and mind open!

▶ Always remember, people are human beings capable of changing to meet their individual needs. Friendship may not come into question where personnel or monetary needs are concerned. **EXAMPLE:** People love each other...get married...save money; then they may divorce and strive to take all that they can from one another. However, they were once loving friends. See the picture?

▶ **Remember:** If a friend wrongs you, it is good to

forgive them, but it is unwise to ever put yourself in a position where your trust may be jeopardized again!

SPECIAL NOTE: *Each checklist was created as a stand-alone guide. Therefore information contained in one checklist may be contained in another.*

CHECKLIST 6
Selecting a Home in a High Crime Area Checklist

If at all possible, do not select a residence in a high crime area. Most often crime is prevalent in these locations due to the illegal drug trade and street gang violence, and is often times made the home of former prisoners when they are released from incarceration. Also, in many cases personal finances and housing discrimination may dictate where a person resides; therefore, when life circumstance mandate people live in high crime communities they must consider using the following checklist to assist them in enhancing personal protection.

Actions/Tips:

► Again, if at all possible, do not reside in a high crime neighborhood. You will become a victim eventually!

► Strive to select a dwelling disconnected from others homes. This offers more security than does an urban housing development. **NOTE:** This may not make a difference in descent neighborhoods.

► Do not reside on the bottom floor of a project building. It provides criminals easier access. If possible, select an apartment or condo located between the second and sixth floors.

► Check Fire Department (FD) capabilities if you live in a multi-floor facility where the FD may not be able to reach certain floors during a critical incident.

NOTE: In some locations the FD may have trouble accessing floors past the six level of a given facility!

▶ Search for housing that provides adequate exterior lighting (e.g., hallway lighting or street lighting).

▶ Conduct research to determine where the worst part of a given neighborhood is located. Note that either residents or the police department can help in this area. Finally, avoid those locations if possible.

▶ Do not reside in an area where drugs are openly sold. If this is taking place the drug distributors must feel secure. And most often, they may feel secure enough to hurt you without having to worry about repercussions from the police.

▶ Strive to rent facilities that employ security personnel or at least offer protective systems (e.g., walls, fences, alarm systems, close circuit television, combination opening gates, etc.).

▶ Find out what the local laws are for legally obtaining a home fire-arm (gun), mace, or other protective weapon. If you are able to legally obtain such protection, ensure people know you possess the weapon system. By doing this you make yourself a protected (i.e., harder) target which deters criminals. **NOTE:** Ensure your weapons are kept out of the hands of children and/or purchase safety devices to protect children from accidentally harming themselves.

▶ If you like animals, consider buying a dog for protection and/or early warning. Additionally, post a warning sign indicating a home alarm or dog is present.

▶ Consider residing in a community that has fully

implemented the **CPTED** (i.e., Crime Prevention Through Environmental Design) concepts of Natural Surveillance, Natural Access Control, and Territorial Reinforcement to protect the community as outlined by Mr. Timothy D. Crowe in his book titled, "CPTED second edition" [2000].

SPECIAL NOTE: Each checklist was created as a stand-alone guide. Therefore information contained in one checklist may be contained in another.

CHECKLIST 7
Home Security Checklist

If you think devising better plans to secure your home is becoming more important in modern times then utilize the following checklist as a guide to increase security at your residence.

Actions/Tips:

▶ Always be aware of your surroundings, even when you are secure behind the closed doors of your home. Awareness that anything bad can happen at any given time is a key to survival **(Stay Alert – Stay Alive).**

▶ Do not trust anyone you do not know who approaches your home without prior notification. This can include people dressed as professionals (e.g., Preachers, Doctors, Police Officers, etc). This could be a smoke screen and/or disguise.

▶ Consider using the term "Mr." and your last name on your door or mail box, regardless if you are female. Criminals are more likely to attack females.

▶ Ensure your residence has a door peep hole or some type of camera system that allows you to observe visitors from behind a closed door. **NOTE:** Modern observation equipment is sold by numerous local electronics dealers.

▶ If you leave the house (or hotel) for short periods of time, consider leaving the radio or television on because intruders may think the home is occupied.

▶ Do not leave messages on your telephone answering machine indicating you are not at home. It is better to leave messages indicating you are busy and/or away from the phone at the moment.

▶ When you go on vacation, choose a friend or relative to frequently check out your home and report suspicious activity to the police. In addition, it may be wise to have the neighbor pick up your mail to prevent a mail pile-up indicating you are away from your home.

▶ Use good locks and safety devices on your doors and windows.

▶ Never leave your house key with a vehicle mechanic.

▶ If you want them, choose monitored burglar alarm systems wisely, and do business only with a reputable company.

▶ Get to know all your neighbors—learn which ones you can trust.

▶ Consider establishing an intercom system with neighbors you trust. This can be used to call for help if you need it.

▶ Teach your children how to dial 911 for help.

▶ Close your curtains at night and keep exterior lights on.

▶ Be cautious of deliveries to your door, especially if you cannot recall ordering anything.

▶ Instruct your kids to never answer the phone by saying their parents are not home. Have them say something like, *"My parents cannot come to the phone right now."*

▶ Be suspicious, report all suspicious activities to the police and/or neighborhood security service.

▶ If you like animals, consider buying a loud barking dog, preferably not vicious to use as an early warning device.

▶ Be cautious if you use babysitters. Consider testing them by leaving small amounts of money lying around the house. If it comes up missing, do not attempt to get the money back. Just be thankful knowing you have figured the person out. Hidden video cameras can also help you determine trust; but give people a chance by informing them in advance that cameras are covertly placed.

▶ Keep your valuables in a safety deposit box or a safe when stored in the home. Make sure the location is in an unusual hiding place.

▶ Always keep your doors closed & locked and the home alarm set (if available), and especially when home alone or young children are home alone.

▶ Do not invite people you meet over the internet to your home until you have thoroughly checked them out. This type of activity can bring you great harm.

▶ Consider installing esthetically pleasant window securing devices, but make sure you can open them from the inside—you may need to use the window to escape.

▶ Consider purchasing a weapon (i.e., gun, stun gun,

or pepper spray) to provide protection for the family. I highly recommend the purchase of a gun, but ensure your minors can not gain access to it.

▶ Get to know the police officers and/or private security service personnel that patrol your neighborhood. If you have a positive relationship, they may put more effort into checking your residence when you are away.

SPECIAL NOTE: *Each checklist was created as a stand-alone guide. Therefore information contained in one checklist may be contained in another.*

CHECKLIST 8
Walking or Jogging in a High Crime Area Checklist

Consider taking the following precautions when you decide to walk or jog in a high crime area or urban environment. Remember these security awareness tips are helpful in all environments.

Actions/Tips:

▶ Do not jog/run at night unless you reside in a well protected neighborhood (e.g., military installation and/or secured community, etc.).

▶ Do not run down alleyways. Normally this is where bad things happen.

▶ Try to alter the direction you walk or jog—do not become predictable. Someone could be waiting to catch you off guard.

▶ Try to walk or jog in areas people often frequent. Larger crowds offer a form of security (e.g., the Crime Prevention Through Environmental Design [CPTED] concept of Natural Surveillance). People will either help you if the situation arises or deter criminals from assaulting you.

▶ Be cautious when you walk or jog by alley openings. Someone could be waiting around the corner to assault you.

▶ Be cautious when walking or jogging in rural (country) areas. You could run into rapist, racist, or other criminals. You do not want to end up a statistic—e.g., dragged by the end of some evil person's pickup truck as seen in Texas some years ago.

▶ Do not wear jewelry or take large sums of money with you when you walk or jog—this increases your chances of becoming a victim.

▶ Consider walking or running against vehicular traffic—that way you can analyze a situation as it is about to happen and take precautions.

▶ Consider carrying legal firearms, mace, or a stun gun when you walk or jog. This can be used to deter wild animals like dogs as well as humans.

▶ Do not allow strangers to get close enough to you to harm you. Be especially cautious of people asking questions from vehicles, and especially vans. Do not allow them to get close enough to pull you in.

▶ Do not walk or jog in unfamiliar areas. Drive your jogging route first to become familiar with surroundings.

▶ If you are approached by someone you feel is going to harm you, act as if you have lost your mind. Throw your hands in the air and scream out obscenities or yell "fire." Or run to a nearby residence and knock on the door for help, or run into the middle of the street thereby stopping traffic as you sound the alarm. Whatever comes to mind to sound the alarm—do it! Someone may hear you and call for help.

▶ Consider carrying your cell phone and/or enough change to call the police if you suspect suspicious activity.

▶ To be even safer—buy a home exercise machine or join a gym.

▶ Avoid large groups of adolescents (3 or more). Walk or run away from their location. Do not take a chance with juveniles. They commit the most violent crimes in America.

SPECIAL NOTE: Each checklist was created as a stand-alone guide. Therefore information contained in one checklist may be contained in another.

CHECKLIST 9
Communicating With Police Checklist

Citizens that reside in high crime, rural, or urban areas must realize most police officers leave their safe suburban neighborhoods to work in what some see as a "lost-hope" community. Therefore, some police officers might look at their job in a negative manner and see you as the reason they must be present. It is your job to ensure the police officer sees you as an honest and caring person. The only way to achieve that goal is to know your patrol officer personally. Therefore, consider following these recommendations when you communicate with the police.

Actions/Tips:

▶ Speak to the police officers in a friendly manner every chance you get. Always be polite and respectful, regardless of how you actually feel (i.e., displays of anger or aggression will not get you anywhere). Strive to get your family members and friends to do the same thing.

▶ Do not ever speak negatively to a police officer. If you have a problem with them, consult their management. If you are in the right, some form of action may be taken. If military police are involved, rest assure, corrective action will be taken.

▶ Invite the police officer over for lunch occasionally.

This will enable the officer to see you as a decent human being.

▶ Get to know every police officer that patrols your community. Strive to get your family members and friends to do the same thing.

▶ If arrested do not fight back. Only fight back if you know/feel for certain police officers are corrupt and mean to do you harm. Then you must do whatever it takes to survive.

▶ Always help police officers fight crime. Report all suspicious or illegal activity to the police. If you wish to remain anonymous, ensure police officers are knowledgeable of your requirement.

▶ If pulled over for a traffic violation follow these recommended steps:

   ▷ If at night, turn on the vehicle dome light and raise your hands so police can see them (all passengers – night or day). If your windows are tinted, roll them down. The key is to make the policeman feel that you are concerned about their safety.

   ▷ Be polite and respectful. Never bad-mouth a police officer.

   ▷ Upon request, show police officers your driver's license, proof of insurance and vehicle registration. Always have your vehicle documents required by law readily available and up to date. Ensure carried weapons and ammunition are legally maintained and stored in the vehicle according to the law. If you do not, then you are asking for trouble. Do not take unnecessary risk unless you are prepared to accept the consequences!

▷ Stay calm and in control of your words, body language (non-verbal gestures) and emotions. Remember, the police officer writes the ticket or report, and not you. Anything you say can and will most likely be used against you.

▷ Always keep your hands where they can see them. Do not brandish any device that can be mistaken for a weapon. Ensure the palms of your hands are empty and visible to the patrol officer.

▷ Do not run, and do not touch the police officer, because the officer may see either action as a hostile act and utilize deadly force against you.

▷ Do not complain on the scene or tell the police they are wrong or that you are going to file a complaint. If you think they are wrong, just get all the facts and inform the police officer's management as soon as you can. Keep in mind, it is probably best to talk with police management versus the on-duty Police Sergeant, unless the on-duty Police Sergeant is a military/federal government employee, because some (not all) non-military police officers may ignore your complaint altogether.

▷ Always remember the police officer's name and badge number. You will definitely need this for officer verification.

▷ If you feel your rights have been violated, file a written complaint with the police department's internal affairs division or civilian complaint board. If the incident occurs on a military installation, you should first consult the on-duty Military Police Shift Commander or Flight Sergeant.

▷ As thoroughly outlined by comedian **Chris Rock** in his televised HBO show called **"The Chris**

Rock Show", do not allow ignorant, criminal, short-tempered, violent, and/or angry non-caring associates to ride with you in a vehicle where the opportunity exist you can be pulled over by a police officer and have one of these personality types (e.g., lover or friend) create a situation with the police that will become hostile to you. Please remember that making this decision is up to YOU, and you are responsible for whatever occurs—good or bad!

SPECIAL NOTE: *Each checklist was created as a stand-alone guide. Therefore information contained in one checklist may be contained in another.*

CHECKLIST 10
Dealing With Suspected Violent People Checklist

Utilize this checklist when confronted by violent people or to gain knowledge on how to deal with violent people. Please keep in mind, these people may be family members, co-workers, friends, or sports team members, etc. The list goes on and can apply to just about anyone.

Actions/Tips:

▶ Take aggressive action to avoid violent people completely. If you know they are trouble makers and you see them coming down the street—go the other way.

▶ Never participate in arguments with people you think will act violently. Chances are—they will. Try to avoid language that may trigger a hostile response (i.e., Treat people the way you would like to be treated).

▶ If you must communicate with people with violent personalities, ensure you maintain a business/professional only relationship.

▶ If possible, do not participate in gossip channels that belittle people. Discussed conversations may get back to the person and trigger a violent response. **Remember:** The world is round, and eventually what is said on one end, will make it around to the other. *No one needs an enemy since an enemy is not designed and/or created to do you any good!*

▶ Avoid extremely jealous people. Spouses and or mates may become violent because of jealousy. This frame of mind could cause you to hurt others and in the process hurt yourself. People should remember that only the **Creator** owns the individual. Therefore, people are free to do whatever they want, and they only have to answer to God. So, if caught in a "Love Triangle" dispute, you should always take the high road (i.e., resolve the issue non-violently). Conversely, just because your mate exercised their God given freedom to act, does not mean you should lose your freedom by acting in a violent manner. Remember, a lot of people are dead or in jail today because of jealousy! Sure, losing the love of a mate may hurt, but you must press on non-violently. Here are a couple examples of jealousy gone wrong as reported in USA Today's, Across The Nation article dated 30 Jul 99, a Stars & Stripes article dated Feb 2007, and an Air Force Times article dated 30 Jan 12:

▷ **USA TODAY'S PARAPHRASED ARTICLE:** A High school honor student named Jacob Davis was found guilty of 1st-degree murder for killing a classmate named Nick Creson three days before both were to graduate last year. A defense psychologists testified that Davis was depressed because his girlfriend had sex with Creson and was exhausted from juggling his job, romance and school work…and he could be sentenced to life in prison without parole.

▷ **STARS & STRIPES PARAPHRASED ARTICLE:** A jury convicted a man of second-degree domestic assault for shoving a cell phone down his girlfriend's throat. Prosecutors said Marlon

Brando Gill, 25, of Kansas City, forced the cell phone into Melinda Abell's mouth during an argument in December 2005. Gill denied the charge, claiming that she tried to swallow the phone to prevent him from finding out whom she had been calling. Abell, 25, of Blue Springs, was rushed to a hospital where doctors removed the phone....the assault charge carries a sentence of up to seven years in prison.

▷ **AIR FORCE TIMES PARAPHRASED ARTICLE:** *Colonel's Wife Accused of Killing Mistress.* The wife of the director of reserve forces for Air Force Space Command has been accused in the shooting death of a psychiatrist in suburban Kansas City, Mo. Shannon L. O'Roark Griffen, 52, of Granbury, Texas, was charged Jan. 14 in Clay County, Mo., with first-degree murder and armed criminal action in the death of Dr. Irina Puscariu of Gladstone, according to court records. O'Roark Griffin shot Puscariu three times at the psychiatrist's home Jan. 13 after her husband, Col. Roscoe L. Griffin, said he would not end their affair, according to court documents. O'Roark Griffin then called her husband and told him what she had done. Roscoe Griffin called the police, documents state.

▶ Pass these tips on to your family members and associates. Some people never learn unless they learn the hard way. The passing on of knowledge may ease someone's pain.

SPECIAL NOTE: *Each checklist was created as a stand-alone guide. Therefore information contained in one checklist may be contained in another.*

CHECKLIST 11
Selection of Family Doctor
Checklist

Utilize this checklist to select the appropriate family doctor. All people, and especially minorities must realize that there are quite a few hate groups in America where primary members practice medicine. American hate group leaders have positioned people in high places all over the country. These people are referred to in **James MDonald's** book called **"The Turner Diaries"** sold at many gun shows adjacent other hate books as **"Legals".** Now, in the security management profession, criminal minded people or **"Legals"** that hold corporate or federal jobs are referred to as **"Insiders."** These people basically support their hate group (or criminal group) of choice by taking direct action, monetary contribution, or by providing sensitive information—and in doing so, they do not want to be CAUGHT because of family embarrassment, prosecution, or loss of employment. At any rate, no one can be truly trusted during these days and times. All people should be checked out, and especially doctors. They have the capability and opportunity under the guise of trained medical officers to prescribe your death without you ever knowing it. A primary example for all to see is the rapid spread of disease in Third World Countries, and especially African, South Asian and former Soviet Union nations. These nations have done away with the advice of the traditional medicine man and have allowed organizations from all over the world to enter their nations and immunize millions without testing the properties of recommended vaccines; thus, potentially leading to death at a massive rate. The same thing can happen here in the states as has been historically recorded by several Americans. All you have to do is look around, open your eyes, and listen. Some hate group leaders have already openly bragged about their influence in the medical and legal professions. Moreover, now that basically all people worldwide have gained access to guns and can somewhat protect themselves, the use of chemical weapons, and especially biological weapons may become the most effective way to eradicate large populations of people. This is a true threat; therefore, consider taking these considerations:

Actions/Tips:

► Whenever possible, conduct research on the individual you wish to provide your family medical services. Do not make the mistake of thinking just because a doctor is from your cultural group that they are okay. Remember African American doctors and nurses at Tuskegee Institute in Alabama participated in the Syphilis Study that killed hundreds of Blacks (see the Isis Papers under books to read). **NOTE**: It should not come as a surprise to you what humans will do for money and/or recognition.

► Be straight-forward! If the doctor does not hold a trusted position in your line of work then ask the doctor is he/she a member of hate group. If you do not have the courage to ask the question, it is your life you are putting at risk. Understand, most **legals and/or insiders** may never admit to this. Your next step should be to look for facial expressions and other identifying signals (e.g., see SLPC web site for hate-based symbols in effort to efficiently evaluate portraits on the wall, rings, tattoos, etc.).

▶ Never take an experimental drug, and especially when given in the place of older more proven drugs for curable diseases. You should be alarmed, if someone asks you to volunteer for a new drug, when an older more proven drug still cures the disease. I personally would not recommend taking an experimental drug unless you are about to die. In this situation, how can you lose?

▶ If you are imprisoned, do not participate in experimental programs to get your time cut or to receive additional liberties or money. You may receive viral organisms that may be transmitted to your love ones on the outside, thus infecting the entire community. On a negative note, one should think seriously about having a relationship with a person who has been incarcerated until they are properly tested or cleared. They are justifiably considered to be in a high-risk category. They have not yet received these protective measures I am giving to you; therefore, ensure your imprisoned relatives or associates are thoroughly checked out by a reliable doctor when they are released from prison. For instance, outlined below is an article from the "Across The USA" section of the 29 Jul 99, USA Today newspaper that should indicate why:

▷ **USA TODAY PARAPHRASED ARTICLE**: Correctional Medical Systems, the company that provides health care for the Penitentiary of New Mexico, kept inmates from getting the treatment they needed and faked records to cover up its actions, a former physician for the company said in a lawsuit....Roy Kropinak says he was fired for blowing the whistle on "unsafe, unethical, possibly illegal and substandard" medical care for inmates...

▶ Law enforcement and military leadership must continue to ensure experimental drugs are safe before allowing prescription to America's service members and policemen. Their members are depending on them for protection. In addition, we must keep a close eye on military doctors as well. One reason why was clearly communicated by Stars & Stripes in their Feb 2007 article (see below):

▷ **STARS & STRIPES PARAPHRASED ARTICLE**: An Air Force officer accused of raping four men & attempting to rape two others pleaded not guilty Monday at the opening of his court-martial. Capt Devery L. Taylor, former chief of patient administration at the Eglin Regional Hospital, is accused of drugging and raping or trying to rape the men, four of whom were in the military, after meeting them in bars in Pensacola and Okaloosa Island....Taylor faces life in prison without parole.

▶ All Americans must realize; some doctors/scientist world-wide have received promotions and awards for developing viruses and bacteria that kill. It is amazing what humans will do for recognition, hate, and money. The thought of one day having to pay for their sins does not even come into the equation, especially if these people are non-believers or they have a religious faith that motivates or justifies criminal acts against other humans. A good example, are the WW II Nazi & Japanese doctors who ran concentration camps in Europe & Asia. Many of which escaped prosecution and immigrated to the Americas, Africa, and other countries where they continued to receive honorable treatment. And let's not forget Wouter Basson, South Africa's notorious "Dr. Death." According to the Vera Haller, author of the USA TODAY's article, *"S. Africa faces its 'Dr. Death,"* Mr. Basson was under prosecution by the country's Truth and Reconciliation Commission for his participation in Operation Project Coast, which was a chemical and biological warfare program set up and ran in the 1980's and early 1990's. His charges range from assassination to murder (i.e., genocide). One of his charges is that he even planned to distribute poisoned beer at rural bus stops frequented by blacks. Please do not forget that this man is a product of a medical society. Under Apartheid he was probably responsible for the death of thousands! A wise person must consider that Mr. Basson is not alone in a world where thousands of biological doctors and scientist exist, and new professionals are being trained each day.

▶ If you have family members in nursing homes and/or mental institutions, ensure you know what medications they are receiving before they are given to them. They are possibly the largest research group outside of prisons and poor citizens who require subsidized medical aid, etc.

▶ **NOTES TO REMEMBER**: (1) One should truthfully acknowledge that our medical system is a capitalist money making system that has both good and bad qualities. Based on that concept alone, you should realize that if a person is not sick, medical facilities and drug companies could not make money. Citizens should notice that our medical professionals always talk treatment (i.e., continual monetary payments for prescription drugs) and seldom discuss cure (i.e., no more money or visits to doctor). (2) Doctors and/or drug companies most likely will never admit to any medical wrong doing—it would be the ultimate shame, and most likely lead to loss of their livelihoods, law suits, or imprisonment! (3) Americans should not expect to see a cure for AIDS, Cancer, Herpes, Acne, the common cold, or any other major disease in your lifetime. There is still too much hate, deniability, and money to be made on research programs and medications that make symptoms go away for as long as a person can afford an ample resupply. You will probably see animals learn to speak first—at taxpayer expense of course. Our only hope is to elect Presidents or Prime Ministers world-wide with the awareness, intelligence, and courage to say, "Enough is enough" and implement a master plan to rid the nations of disease. I personally, believe it can be done—someday! The question is, "Do you? (4) Biological and chemical agents are the new threat of the world. Diseases developed and produced by scientist worldwide can now be obtained by the general populace over the internet; thus, putting us all in danger! This just goes to show—we as humans will ultimately reap what we sow (see **Attachment 29** of this book, and review specifically read books 6, 7, 8, 10, 11, & 12).

▶ Please inform your family members and associates. Additionally, just do not take my recommendations alone, do your research and read the books of others who are trying to alert you.

SPECIAL NOTE: *Each checklist was created as a stand-alone guide. Therefore information contained in one checklist may be contained in another.*

CHECKLIST 12
Celebrity Dating Protection Checklist

In recent years, many people have set in front of their televisions and watched horrendous stories about covert celebrity relationships resulting in unplanned pregnancies, inappropriate sexual request, and sexual assaults *supposedly* committed by celebrities like Mike Tyson, Brett Farve, Kobe Bryant, Ben Roethlisberger, and even more distinguished superstars like Bill Cosby. However, as a 30-year military police officer and security manager it is difficult for me to believe these incidents and/or date rapes actually took place without prompt police reporting, immediate medical examinations or other forms of physical evidence. Yet, all these stories made the news and government prosecutors and police agencies were called into action. So, the question is, **"How could these offenses have been avoided?"**

Well, wealthy celebrities must thoroughly understand the world they live in. The modern world is basically about making money by any means necessary, regardless of the way! Even the average American realizes many frivolous law suits are initiated by citizens everyday against wealthy people or organizations in effort to enrich themselves, and these law suits are fought in courts staffed by countless employees who also make money off of these court appearances (e.g., Judges, lawyers, bailiffs, court room maintenance employees, court room recorders, etc.). **Therefore, wealthy celebrities, military personnel, and regular citizens should consider taking**

these steps to prevent becoming involved in date rape or sexual assaults:

Actions/Tips:

▶ Realize the *predominant reason* a love interest has found a way to enter your life is that you are a wealthy celebrity, and if a positive relationship develops, there exist a possibility that they may become a married partner, and therefore share in your wealth.

▶ Realize that you must thoroughly communicate with potential sex partners and discuss all possible sexual relations that may/may not occur. Doing this will normally prevent any negative act from occurring, and especially if the female's response is, "Nothing is going to happen tonight!"

▶ In modern times, it might be wise to have your mate (and/or one night stand) sign a legal document authorizing their adult participation in any sexual activity both partners agree upon. In addition, it might be wise to install electronic observation equipment to oversee and record sexual relations as long as both partners agree to this activity.

▶ If all else fails, either because of ineffective communication skills, or your hotel does not have video equipment, or you do not have video equipment, or you do not have the appropriate legal forms, then it will be wise to carry out the following procedures:

▷ *Ensure you treat your date with utmost **Dignity and Respect**.* Realize the greatest thing a female can do for a male is to allow the male inside her most private space; thereby, providing a male the same pleasure "Eve" most likely gave "Adam". Therefore, women deserve to be treated by a male (e.g., rich, middle class, or poor) with the utmost *Dignity and Respect* throughout their relationship. Treat her like your best friend until she departs your company, and ensure she departs your company in style since many males do have the funds to make this a positive reality!

▷ If you partake in sexual relations, ensure people see you in a public forum before you part ways. The best thing to do is go to breakfast in a public setting, or walk her past the door man and kiss her as she gets into a taxi (or limo), take her home yourself, or take pictures of her eating the breakfast you prepared. Additionally, always remember to give a public departure kiss before you depart the area. **Here is why this is important:**

  ▸ *Who goes to breakfast with their rapist?*

  ▸ *Who is driven home by their rapist?*

  ▸ *Who gives their rapist a public morning farewell kiss?*

  ▸ *Who eats breakfast prepared by their rapist?*

  ▸ **NOTE:** *All would be good questions for a lawyer in court!*

▸ Realize that either rich or poor, some angry mates understand the legal system when it comes to males versus females in sexual assault cases, and deviant people will lie in order to get even with mates they are angry with. As a policeman, I have seen these fabrications told on many occasions. And even without an eyewitness or substantial physical evidence, the male is basically seen as guilty until proven innocent. Such is life in America—Americans tend to believe negative events easier than they believe positive events. For example, in America a person can say, *"I think John Doe is a great person"* and some person on the other end of the conversation will say, *"Well, I heard otherwise."* Normally if a negative comment is originally stated, someone in the audience will respond by saying, *"I'd better watch out then."*

▷ These are key steps wealthy males and the average person should consider when they engage in the dating game, and especially with women they do not know very well.

▶ **NOTE 1:** Some sexual assault (date rape) claims are truthful, and some are not. Some sexual assaults exist primarily among rich and poor people, and some exist against members of the same economic strata. Some sexual assaults are also complete fabrications made by lovers who want to get even with males they are angry with. Therefore, all actions should be taken to prevent citizens from becoming involved in an embarrassing court appearances where even parents (non-victims) will have to endure the pain. Be wise, and do not allow this to happen. **Only love those, who freely agree to love you!**

▶ **NOTE 2:** Please realize that you can be hurt emotionally, physically, publicly, and financially when you foolishly enter into unwise intimate personal relationships. Therefore, in modern times, many dishonest and extremely attractive people may pursue wealthy males strictly for financial gain and there are many ways to obtain their goals (i.e., money). Yes, someone could say a wealthy person sexually assaulted them, or they become purposely impregnated, or they can even become a spouse who later divorces a millionaire per se, and is awarded millions as quite often observed in the divorces of wealthy people (e.g., movie stars, professional athletes, and/or professional businessmen, etc).   So, wealthy people must be extremely wise when they partake in intimate relationships and marriages. My best advice is to take whatever steps possible to protect yourself from unwanted pregnancies (and diseases), striving to marry people you know extremely well or already have money, developing a prenuptial agreement, and/or just staying single and safely dating. If not, you could become the next victim of a multi-million dollar law suit or lose millions to a spouse who probably really did not love you in the first place. Moreover, these spouses who may have come into the relationship with little are now living like millionaires without having put in any unusual work (i.e., without winning basketball championships, Super Bowls, or staring in any Hollywood movies, etc.). The truth is; when one is married to a millionaire, chances are, the only physical thing they will probably have to do is clean their body and put on expensive cloths; but because some adult did not think properly, some lover now has it **"Made in the Shade"** so-to-speak.

▶ **Please use your mind and protect all that you have earned!** Dishonest people are everywhere; and believe me—their skills are well rehearsed!

SPECIAL NOTE: Each checklist was created as a stand-alone guide. Therefore information contained in one checklist may be contained in another.

CHECKLIST 13
Staying Clear of Dangerous Lovers Checklist

Please utilize this checklist to stay clear of potential lovers who see you as an owned object, regardless if you are married or not, and will harm you if they perceive you are moving away from the relationship or cheating. This subject should not take much motivation to get the message across because Americans read about these horrendous love crimes everyday in newspapers or hear about them on television. Additionally, many Americans who dated in middle school and high school can attest to being involved in a relationship that became hostile towards its natural end. These relationships normally led to harsh words, fights, and sometimes murder as vividly described by these two paraphrased 2007 Stars & Stripes articles (see below):

TX, HUNTSVILLE: An ex-boyfriend shot and killed a 20-year old Sam Houston State cheerleader before killing himself while her three roommates were in the same apartment, police said. Rachel Pendray, a pre-nursing major and sorority member at Sam Houston State, died from three or four gunshot wounds....Her roommates told school officials that Jake Taylor... stopped by the apartment to see Pendray....then the two went into a room together....then roommates heard gun shots and found the two dead.

MO, INDEPENDENCE: A jury convicted a man of second degree domestic assault for shoving a cell phone down his girlfriend's throat. Prosecutors said

Marlon Brando Gill, 25, of Kansas City, forced the cell Phone into Melinda Abell's mouth during an argument in December 2005. Gill denied the charge, claiming that she tried to swallow the phone to prevent him from finding out whom she had been calling. Abell, 25, of Blue Springs, was rushed to a hospital where doctors removed the phone...doctors said she nearly died of a blocked airway.

WA, SEATTLE: Prosecutors filed a second degree murder charge Thursday against Johnnie Lee Wiggins, who is accused in the beating death of his girlfriend, Prudence Hockley, in Seattle on **Christmas Eve, 2011**. Investigators believe Johnnie Lee Wiggins beat and killed 55-year-old Prudence Hockley outside her home in the 300 block of NW 74th Street. *Hockley was a mother, a teacher, and into fitness.* Friends say she met and started dating Wiggins after they met at a gym. Wiggins is a championship body builder. Court documents show Wiggins went looking for Hockley at her home Christmas Eve. Wiggins told police he only wanted to deliver a gift and didn't mean for "anyone to get hurt" but then he spotted a man leaving through her back door and that's when he told investigators, things "just went bad from there." That man, a friend Hockley had over, told police that Hockley panicked when Wiggins showed up and told him to leave out her back door. He said as he left, he heard a commotion and Hockley's teenage daughter yelling, and then he found Hockley on the ground, bleeding. She died the next day; the medical examiner said she had multiple fractures to her head and face. Police called Wiggins (also a Georgia convicted felon) and he later turned himself in with an attorney.

Now, these types of crime come as no surprise to me, since I have seen these critical incidents repeated quite often. Not to mention, American prisons are full of people who have committed similar acts of rage due to jealousy, but why should Americans continue to allow themselves to fall victim to such nonsense? Well, love triangle crimes are a major American problem that national leaders have not effectively attempted to resolve since there is still a strong societal and/or mental assumption that a person physically owns another human (i.e., their mate) and is responsible for correcting them or their new lovers.

Therefore, consider using these recommendations to prevent **YOU** from becoming a victim of a relationship gone extremely bad?

Actions/Tips:

▶ Realize people are free to make whatever decisions they want as far as romantic relationships go. They can either love you on a given day, and change their minds the next day. If they are adults, then they only have to answer to the Creator, if they even believe in a Creator. Plus, just because a person decides someone will not be their long lasting mate, does not give a person the right to hurt or murder these people just because they are angry.

▶ Realize now, that if a mate determines your romantic relationship is over; then you should walk away non-violently, just as if an employer released you from a job. Please take note, that under these circumstances most humans would be emotionally hurt, but people must see the positive side of such a scenario. Why should you have to force someone to love you—realize there are more fish in the sea, and the seas are connected to every continent on the Earth. And when I use the word "fish", I am not referring to Catfish, but actually Red Snapper, Salmon, and Trout—get the picture? Maybe your true love is standing by!

▶ When you meet a new partner, it is wise to explore the background of the potential mate by asking some key questions that will hopefully provide desired information to help evaluate if a person should stay committed to the relationship. **NOTE:** Please do not shy away from this process. If you do, you may be putting your life in jeopardy; therefore, here are some sample questions:

> ▷ If you are in a relationship, do you believe that you own your mate like you own a car or house?

> ▷ If your mate decided that he/she was not interested in you anymore, would you attempt to hurt them in any way or form (e.g., physical, legally, or financially)?

> ▷ Have you ever been in an abusive relationship?

> ▷ Has your father or mother ever been abusive in their relationship?

> ▷ Have you ever been in a physical altercation with your mate? If so, why?

> ▷ How would you feel if your love interest after a long period of time decided to break the relationship off with you, and take some other mate? What would you do if involved in such a situation?

> ▷ Do you believe that people who have entered

into a loving relationship should ever use harsh or discouraging words towards one another?

▷ Have you ever served time in jail and/or prison? If so, why?

▷ Have you ever participated in a violent crime where some person was hurt?

▷ Have you ever been seen by a psychologist or spent time in a mental institution?

▷ **NOTE:** These are just a few questions you should consider utilizing to evaluate the mental standing of your potential mate. Any answer should be self-explanatory to the average American. Either you take time to do this, or you do not; but if things go wrong, you will surely wish you had!

► Furthermore, just because you are extremely attracted to someone, or you are in dire need to be held/loved by some person, does not release you from the adult responsibility to protect your life! Many humans have fallen into violent relationships for these two primary reasons, as a minimum! Do not let it be you! Please conduct research and/or outline agreed upon rules at the beginning of relationships. Yes—make two list of relationship rules, then discuss them as a team!

► Finally, a person must protect their love ones from criminals. It is not wise to turn the other cheek and do nothing in a world where the average criminal would perceive this response as a sign of weakness and become more violent. Yet—it is never wise to fight over the "LOVE of a Mate" when they should love you unconditionally and without force. Therefore, if a mate does not love you anymore, then let them freely walk away since no one owns them!

SPECIAL NOTE: *Each checklist was created as a stand-alone guide. Therefore information contained in one checklist may be contained in another.*

CHECKLIST 14
Travel Briefing Checklist

In the past many Americans and others have encountered criminal activity when traveling away from their neighborhoods, cities, states, and/or nations. Therefore, I recommend travelers consider using security recommendations outlined in this checklist to help mitigate criminal threats.

Actions/Tips:

► If possible, travel in civilian clothing, not corporate attire or in military uniforms.

► Keep a low profile. Do not draw attention to yourself.

► Remove US government decals and insignia from luggage, jackets, vehicles, etc to establish a low profile preferably not American.

► When in foreign countries, try your best not to wear clothing that readily identifies you as an American.

► Always vary your times and routes—avoid being predictable.

► Use different entrances and exits to buildings so one does not develop a pattern.

► Know your routes, always stay alert.

► Know the location of safe havens (police, hospital, embassy, etc.,).

► Be alert for surveillance activity.

► Look for suspicious persons, vehicles, and packages.

► Avoid trips to remote areas because these locations may be present higher risk.

► Travel on major thoroughfares; and avoid side streets and alleys.

► When overseas or unfamiliar areas, it is not wise to travel alone; yet, strive to travel in small groups (size: 2-5 people). Larger groups present harder targets to criminals.

► Park vehicles in secure areas.

► Search vehicles before use. **See attachment 15**.

► Always keep vehicles locked.

► **HOT!** Do not store sensitive or valuable material in the vehicle (personal or rental) because there is a high chance it may be stolen!

► Ensure vehicles are mechanically sound in effort to prevent breakdowns.

► Try to obtain communication equipment for vehicles in case of emergency (e.g., cell phones).

► Do not disclose details about daily activities to strangers.

► Wisely consider not stopping for strangers and/or offering any assistance to limit risk.

► Keep hotel rooms locked, and neat in effort to detect changes in the room.

► Do not permit repair or delivery personnel in your room; unless you...

▷ Verify the identity of such individuals via hotel front desk, or

▷ Arrange appointments for them.

▷ **NOTE:** Monitor the activities of your MAID.

► Identify emergency exits at hotels.

► Avoid establishments that cater exclusively to Americans. If overseas, there is a good chance you may become a target.

► Stay in secured areas of airports since criminals will have less access to you.

► If possible, limit time near airline counters.

► Do not hand-carry classified or sensitive documents unless absolutely critical.

► If assigned drivers are required, check them out before departure. Next, determine if they know specific procedures to counter a car-jacking or terrorist vehicle assault. If they do not, ensure they are briefed and or trained properly.

► Plan to switch pre-assigned rooms upon arrival at foreign hotels.

► Do not leave laptop computers in your hotel room insecure. Take these items with you or secure them; yet, never leave them in a vehicle either since the hotel room is probably safer!

► If in the military, travel with your civilian passport unless you are required by military rules to utilize your US government passport. It is a good thing for military personnel to possess both types of passports so you have flexibility. **NOTE 1**: Possessing a Diplomatic passport may even offer more protection; and especially when communicating with foreign police. **NOTE 2:** If for some reason your passport is stolen, immediately contact the U.S. Department of State Passport Services via email (e.g., travel.gov) or telephone the Consular Lost/Stolen Passport Section via the Internet or telephone.

SPECIAL NOTE: Each checklist was created as a stand-alone guide. Therefore information contained in one checklist may be contained in another.

CHECKLIST 15
Personal Vehicle Security Checklist

Consider using this checklist to thoroughly inspect your vehicle during periods of increased threat or if you suspect vehicle tampering. This checklist can also be used as a guide to train others.

Actions/Tips:

▶ Visually check parking area for intruders or suspicious items.

▶ If possible, search the vehicle in pairs. Start searching the area around the vehicle in a clock like motion looking for bomb making debris (e.g., wires and such).

▶ Check exterior of the vehicle for any fingerprints, smudges, or other signs of tampering. To make the check easier—leave vehicles dusty and dirty, so you can see new fingerprints and such.

▶ Check electronic tamper devices, if installed. A cheaper option is to use transparent tape on the hood, trunk, gas gap, and doors to alert you to any tampering.

▶ Check underneath the car, under the fender wells, under the bumpers, and exhaust pipe for any foreign objects, loose wire, etc.

▶ Examine wheel lug nuts and the tires for stress marks and any evidence of tampering.

▶ Check the interior of the vehicle. Use extreme caution. Determine if the doors have been manipulated. Open doors (passenger doors first) slowly, just a very small amount (1-2 inches or less), LOOK, and then feel gently with your fingers for a trip wire. If none are found, the door can then be opened all the way. Always look inside for suspicious packages or bomb debris. Do not touch anything yet. Look at the carpet and under seats for suspicious packages. Carefully inspect ashtrays, under the dash, the glove compartment, air ducts, and sun visors and mirrors for signs of tampering.

▶ Check under the hood and in the trunk. Use caution when searching. Open hood/trunk slowly, just a very small amount (1-2 inches or less), LOOK, and then feel gently with your fingers for a trip wire. If none are found, the compartment can then be opened all the way. Look for items not normally seen under the hood, and remember to check the air filter. Pay special attention to the spark plug wire, the distributor, the ignition area, and exhaust manifold. Check the trunk for out of place items. Use same method as for opening the hood.

▶ If necessary, take the following steps to harden your vehicle:

  ▷ Lock the hood with an additional lock and ensure the factory latch is located inside the vehicle.

  ▷ Have oversized mirrors installed and keep visors down.

  ▷ Utilize a locking gas gap.

  ▷ Put two bolts through the exhaust pipe, perpendicular to one another. This prevents the insertion of explosive devices in the tail pipe.

  ▷ Use steel-belted radial tires.

▷ Install an intrusion alarm system and an extra battery.

▷ Post Security on your vehicle if absolutely necessary.

▷ In high-threat areas or if you know for certain someone is attempting to hurt you, it may be appropriate to:

  ► *Install car armor (only if you have the funds).*

  ► *Have an interior escape latch installed in the trunk.*

  ► *Use fog lights (provides better visibility).*

  ► *Install bullet-resistant glass (only if you have the funds).*

► **REMEMBER:** In foreign countries it might be prudent to search all cars, especially rental cars. Recommend switching rental cars if one is specifically assigned when you arrive at the contracting company. In addition, when leaving your vehicle conduct a visual scan, and commit to memory the location of items in, near, and around your vehicle. This will aid in detecting explosive devices or someone tampering with your vehicle. **NOTE:** All of these security tips become especially important if you are a high ranking government official traveling abroad representing America!

SPECIAL NOTE: Each checklist was created as a stand-alone guide. Therefore information contained in one checklist may be contained in another.

CHECKLIST 16
Ground Transportation Security Checklist

Consider using this checklist to provide safety briefings to family members and associates that use government or rental vehicles in foreign locations.

Actions/Tips:

▶ Vehicles:

▷ Select a plain car, minimize the "rich American " look.

▷ Consider not using a government car that announces American ownership or GOV (i.e., Government Operated Vehicle).

▷ Safeguard keys.

▷ Keep vehicle in good repair; ensure tires have sufficient tread.

▷ Keep gas tank at least ½ full at all times.

▶ Parking:

▷ Park in well-lighted areas.

▷ Always lock your car.

▷ If possible, do not leave the car on the street overnight or during the day for extended periods of time (even if police patrols or substations are present).

▷ Do not allow entry to the trunk unless you are there to watch.

▷ Never get out without checking for suspicious persons. If in doubt, drive away.

▷ Leave only the ignition key with parking attendants.

▷ Never leave garage doors open or unlocked.

▷ Use a remote garage door opener if available. Enter and exit your car in the security of a closed garage.

▷ **NOTE:** When forced to park along the road side in foreign countries, it might be wise to ask vagrants to watch your car and tip them up front—especially if their hands are already out. If not, they may be the ones that harm you in some way or form.

▶ On The Road:

▷ Check area for suspicious activity before leaving the building.

▷ Check vehicle for suspicious objects before entering.

▷ Vary travel routes and avoid late night trips.

▷ If possible, travel with companions or in convoy.

▷ Avoid isolated roads and dark alleys.

▷ Know locations of safe-havens along routes of routine travel.

▷ When driving use seat-belts, lock doors, and keep windows closed.

▷ Do not get boxed in; allow a minimum 8-foot interval between vehicles (VERY IMPORTANT SAFEGUARD). This will give you the necessary room required to escape terrorist ambushes and/or prevent car-jacking attempts.

▷ Be alert while driving.

▷ Know how to react if surveillance is suspected or confirmed.

  ▸ *Circle the block for confirmation of surveillance.*

  ▸ *Do not stop or take other actions that could lead to a violent confrontation.*

  ▸ *Do not drive home since you may be followed.*

  ▸ *Get description of car and its occupants.*

  ▸ *Go to nearest safe haven and report the incident to authorities.*

▶ Recognize events that can signal the start of an attack, such as:

  ▷ Cyclist falling in front of your car.

  ▷ Flagman or workman stopping your car.

  ▷ Fake police or government checkpoint.

  ▷ Disabled vehicle or accident victims on the road.

  ▷ Unusual detours.

  ▷ An accident in which your car is struck (tactic often used in US)

  ▷ Cars or pedestrian traffic that box you in preventing escape.

  ▷ Attractive female looking for a ride or starting a conversation.

  ▷ Sudden activity or gunfire.

  ▷ Know what to do if under attack in a vehicle.

    ▸ *Without subjecting yourself to harm, draw attention by sounding the horn.*

    ▸ *Put another vehicle between you and your pursuer.*

▸ *Execute immediate turn and escape, jump curb at 30-45 degree angle, 35 mph maximum.*

▸ *Ram blocking vehicle if necessary.*

▸ *Go to closest safe haven.*

▸ **Do not just sit there in a state of shock. You will surely be killed. You must take steps to get out of the attack (or kill) zone.**

▸ *Report incident to nearest law enforcement organization.*

▸ Commercial Buses, Trains, Contracted Drivers, and Taxis:

▷ Vary mode of commercial transportation.

▷ Select busy stops.

▷ Do not always use the same taxi company—if possible, do not ride alone, especially in large cities located in foreign countries.

▷ Do not let someone you do not know direct you to a specific taxi.

▷ Ensure the taxi is licensed and has safety equipment (seat belts at minimum).

▸ *If a picture is provided, ensure face of driver and picture on license are the same.*

▷ Obtain *local city map* from the Hotel and locate where you plan to go, then show perspective taxi drivers you know where you are located in the city, and where you need to travel.

▸ *Select a marked taxi positioned adjacent the Hotel, but you must expect to pay a higher fee; yet, marked taxis flagged down on the streets will be less expensive but your safety risk may be higher.*

▷ When traveling by taxi, avoid discussing sensitive business or personal issues. You could be setting yourself up for blackmail or possibly disclosing protected information. Assume taxi drivers speak fluent English even if they say they do not.

▷ Try to travel with a companion (e.g., utilize two person security policy).

▷ If possible, specify the route you want the taxi to follow and use the hotel city map to accomplish this task.

▷ If using contracted transportation, ensure your assigned driver is checked out before getting into the vehicle. Several Americans have been murdered by terrorist organizations while riding in contracted vehicles and the drivers were not even touched.

NOTE: Flagging vehicles down on the streets to obtain cheap transportation in some nations is a way of life, and the security aid in doing this is that potential passengers are unpredictable. They can show up on the street and just raise a hand and some vehicle will stop and transport them to some location for a predetermined price. Of course, this activity is not seen or recommended in America, since in our nation we have an abundance of crazies that seek to do people harm! However, if you are in Russia, this is a mode of transportation that is utilized quite often by the general populace, yet I only recommended this mode of transportation for experienced Americans or foreigners (only); but even still, utilize your city hotel map to indicate your present location and where you want to go. In addition, before you get into a vehicle, ensure the price of the ride is established up front. This will prevent arguments once you have reached your destination.

SPECIAL NOTE: *Each checklist was created as a stand-alone guide. Therefore information contained in one checklist may be contained in another.*

CHECKLIST 17
Hotel Security Checklist

Consider using this checklist to enhance security when using hotels in America and overseas. Note that all recommendations should be based on the locally assumed threat to your individual person. In places like the Middle East and certain South American nations, Americans should always assume the threat to their personal security is high.

Actions/Tips:

▶ If you are in the military stay at DD facilities whenever possible.

▶ Avoid staying in hotels with distinctively American names or predominantly American guest; unless the hotel has been recommended by US Embassy personnel—otherwise, you could become a target!

▶ Make reservations in two or more hotels; and if allowed, use an assumed or modified name, and consider changing rooms upon arrival.

▶ Avoid selecting street-level rooms, terrace-level rooms with direct access to hotel grounds, or stairwells; Strive to select interior rooms located between the second and six floors. Making this decision will make it more difficult for street criminals to enter your room, and you do not want to be so high that the fire departments in small countries cannot reach your floor.

▶ Retain control over all luggage upon arrival in a hotel lobby. Keep your luggage locked.

▶ When in a hotel, note emergency exits and potential escape routes.

▶ Vary your pattern of entering and leaving your hotel.

▶ Do not discuss travel plans over hotel phones.

▶ When in foreign countries use extra caution in hotel lobbies and other public places where bombings or armed attacks may take place. Do your business and quickly move on!

▶ I recommend not asking bellboys and other strangers in hotel lobbies for directions to specific places you intend to go—use the information desk.

▶ Do not conduct official business or meet casual acquaintances in your temporary living quarters; consider not divulging the location of your hotel room and/or quarters.

▶ Discourage efforts to enter your room while you are gone by preserving a "lived-in" look in your room (i.e., leaving on lights, TV, radio, etc.).

▶ Keep your room neat so you can readily detect any changes.

▶ Check hallways for suspicious personnel or packages prior to exiting the elevator or your room.

▶ I recommend you do not use an elevator, public subway, or public bus occupied by large groups of adolescents, and especially when you just do not feel comfortable. Remember; adolescents are responsible for most violent crimes in America and many places throughout the world.

▶ Do not allow packages to be delivered directly to your room or pick up packages you did not request. They could contain a letter bomb, or it could be part of a scheme to harm you.

▶ Do not leave or store sensitive documents in your room, and especially your laptop computer. Lock these items up or ask a person you know and trust in another occupied room to watch over it. Always apply access security codes to gain access to laptop data.

▶ Unexpected mail left for you at the desk or slipped under the door of your room should be viewed with suspicion. **NOTE:** I recommend not using hotel room safes to store important material since many of these safes can be readily opened by staff.

SPECIAL NOTE: Each checklist was created as a stand-alone guide. Therefore information contained in one checklist may be contained in another.

CHECKLIST 18
Defensive Flying Security Checklist

As many Americans already know, air travel anywhere in the world pose security problems different from those of ground transportation. Here are some simple precautions that can reduce the hazards of a terrorist assault and/or other criminal incidents. Consider using this checklist to brief family members and associates prior to embarking on airline trips.

Actions/Tips:

► Making Travel Arrangements:

▷ If you can, contact state department officials or the in-country Embassy Regional Security Officer to get a threat briefing prior to traveling to a high-risk area.

▷ If possible, use US flag carrier aircraft when traveling.

▷ Avoid scheduling flights through high-risk locations.

▷ If in the military, do not use rank or military address on tickets, travel documents, or hotel reservations.

▷ Select a window seat because they offer more protection since aisle seats are closer to the hijacker's movements up and down the aisle.

▷ Select seats towards the middle and upper rear of the aircraft primarily because these seats are further from the center of the hostile action which is often near the cockpit or final row of aircraft seats. However, keep in mind that the final rows of aircraft is where terrorist rear security elements may be covertly seated.

▷ Also, seats at an emergency exit may provide an opportunity to escape.

▶ Personal Identification:

▷ Do not discuss US government affiliation with anyone. NOTE: If you are military returning from the Middle East in uniform on U.S. contracted aircraft this security step is not required.

▷ You must have proper identification to show airline and immigration officials.

▷ Consider use of a tourist passport (if you have one) with necessary visas mandated by the country you are visiting.

▷ If you use a tourist passport, consider placing your official passport, military ID, travel orders and related documents in your checked luggage, not in your wallet or briefcase.

▷ If you must carry these documents on your person, select a hiding place on board the aircraft to 'ditch' them in case of a hijacking.

▷ Do not carry classified documents unless they are ABSOLUTELY mission essential.

▶ Luggage (attempt to conceal knowledge that you are an American):

▷ Use plain, civilian luggage; and if you are in the military and it is possible, avoid military-looking bags (i.e., A-3 bags, duffel bags, etc.).

▷ Remove all military patches, logos, or decals from your luggage and briefcase.

▷ Ensure luggage tags do not indicate your government status.

▷ Do not carry classified documents unless they are absolutely essential and secured properly. Do not check-in luggage containing classified information—it is against the law!

▶ Clothing:

▷ Travel in conservative civilian clothing when using commercial transportation.

▷ Strive not to wear distinct American items such as cowboy hats or boots, baseball caps, American logo T-shirts, jackets, or sweatshirts.

▷ Wear a long-sleeved shirt or bandage if you have a visible US affiliated tattoo since there is a risk you may become a target.

▶ Precautions at the Airport:

▷ Arrive early and watch for suspicious activity.

▷ Look for nervous passengers who maintain eye contact with others from a distance. Observe what people are carrying. Note behavior not consistent with that of others.

▷ No matter where you are in the terminal, identify objects suitable for cover in the event of attack. Pillars, trash cans, luggage, large planters, counters, and furniture can provide protection.

▷ Do not linger near open public areas. Quickly transit insecure ticket counters, waiting rooms, commercial shops, and restaurants. This is especially a key recommendation for military personnel who must fly out of airports in Seattle and/or Los Angeles where large groups of military personnel may congregate at airline counters directly adjacent streets where vehicle borne improvised explosives devices (i.e., VBIEDs) can be easily employed.

▷ Avoid processing with known target groups.

▷ Avoid secluded areas that provide concealment for attackers.

▷ Be aware of unattended baggage anywhere in the terminal.

▷ Observe the baggage claim area from a distance. Consider not retrieving your bags until the crowd clears.

▷ Proceed to customs lines at the edge of the crowd.

▷ Report suspicious activity to airport security personnel.

▷ Travel in small groups (2-5). If traveling with a large group, split into smaller groups of two to five when in public places.

▶ Actions to take during Modern Aircraft Highjacking Situations:

▷ Realize the modern terrorist may want to use the aircraft as an explosive device as witnessed in the American 9/11 terrorist act.

▷ Consider taking immediate steps to protect your life!

▸ Attempt to overtake the intruder by any means necessary

▸ Team up with another passenger to overtake the intruder

▸ Take steps to ensure the intruder does not gain access to the Cockpit

▷ Remember; you must protect your life

because failure to take action will normally lead to certain death!

SPECIAL NOTE: *Each checklist was created as a stand-alone guide. Therefore information contained in one checklist may be contained in another.*

CHECKLIST 19
Hostage Survival Briefing Checklist

Hopefully, becoming a hostage never occurs in your life. But if it does, please consider becoming familiar with recommendations in this checklist in order to enhance your survival during a hostage situation. Remember, the key to readiness/survival rests with the individual and his or her ability to apply their training.

Actions/Tips:

► Ensure that your personal affairs are in order so you are prepared for any emergency/contingency:

▷ Keep financial matters current. If needed, start allotments.

▷ Make plans in case of an emergency. Discuss long term matters such as children's education and possible relocation.

▷ Make arrangements to aid your family in an emergency. Secure the assistance of relatives or friends to help the family during a crisis.

▷ Ensure key documents are up to date. Make sure your will is current and that appropriate powers of attorney are drawn up.

► Make sure you have necessary medication when traveling.

► (If possible), do not carry classified or sensitive documents.

► Remember, the moment of capture and release are

the most critical and dangerous periods (e.g., initial criminal detainment period, and then the rescue period conducted by responding police). Be alert and safe!

▶ The decision to resist apprehension or surrender must be weighed against the danger of overwhelming negative odds. **IMPORTANT NOTE:** If you are about to be abducted by people you suspect of being in some type of hate group, it may be wise to attempt escape by any means necessary. Because of their ideology, chances are they will seriously hurt or kill you.

▶ Be prepared to explain any documents, telephone numbers, etc.

▶ Sudden movements or noise may produce a violent response.

▶ Maintain composure; and recognize what is happening around you.

▶ Expect the use of blindfolds, gags, and re-straining devices.

▶ Do not resist or struggle; this could result in greater violence.

▶ Stay alert; occupy your mind by focusing on sounds, movement, etc.

▶ Engage in memory exercises.

▶ Request reading and writing materials—this will help you beat time and boredom.

▶ Be prepared for harsh living conditions:

▷ Loss of privacy.

▷ Inadequate food and environmental conditions.

▷ Inadequate toilet facilities.

▷ **NOTE:** Wherever they place you, attempt to keep the area as clean as possible. A clean area will be better for you both mentally and physically. Plus, your captors will see you as human and hopefully will treat you as such.

► Let captors know of any medical condition and request medication.

► Establish an exercise program (this will definitely reduce stress).

► Participate freely in photo sessions if conducted (this may indicate you are still alive).

► Establish rapport with your captors:

▷ Let them know you are human.

▷ Do not try to deceive them or support their cause.

▷ Show them pictures of your family members in effort to become more human.

▷ Do not present the ugly American attitude foreign terrorists have grown to despise.

▷ Do not talk politics or religion; and remember, the more time that elapses, the greater your chances of survival.

► Learn to control fear—you will enable yourself to think more clearly and maintain your self-esteem.

► Remember to leave fingerprints on just about everything you come in contact with. You may be moved from place to place, and if you leave fingerprints, it may lead authorities to valuable clues.

▶ Remember to always be prepared for rescue, and if a rescue attempt takes place accomplish the following actions: (1) Immediately drop to the floor, (2) Do not pick up a weapon—police may think you are one of the abductors, (3) Do not assist rescue forces, (4) Expect to be handled roughly, (4) Avoid sudden movements, (5) Do not attempt to run, and finally (5) Thank your Creator if you get out safely!

▶ Follow these procedures during the release operation: (1) Pay attention to police instructions, (2) Avoid sudden movements—police are looking for abductors attempting to fit in with hostages and may react aggressively towards you, (3) Do not panic, and (4) Do not attempt to run—or make any sudden movements as outlined above.

SPECIAL NOTE: Each checklist was created as a stand-alone guide. Therefore information contained in one checklist may be contained in another.

CHECKLIST 20
Emergency First Aid Checklist

When residing in a high crime or urban environment the chances of encountering a person who has been violently injured and in need of emergency attention is great. Therefore, it may become extremely important to know some basic first aid skills. You should **first** increase your knowledge by obtaining Cardiopulmonary Resuscitation (CPR) and first aid training through your local Red Cross facility or nearby hospital. Recommend use of the attached checklist to re-familiarize yourself with appropriate steps to take when conducting emergency first aid.

Actions/Tips:

▶ Conduct an area survey to ensure the scene is safe!

▶ Check victims with most life threatening injuries first! These are normally the most quiet people. Then check those with minor injuries. Utilize your **ABC's (Airway-Breathing-Circulation)** when helping the injured; try not to touch blood—wear medical gloves; and continuously re-assure victims by talking and keeping them awake.

▷ Check for open **airway** - Position victim on back and use the head tilt/chin lift measure taught in local first aid courses; if spine an injury is suspected, open the airway using the Trauma Jaw Thrust method without moving the neck. If needed, clear the airway with a finger sweep to remove any foreign body obstruction. If the patient is having seizures, do not put anything in the mouth, unless it is a bite stick.

▷ **Breathing** - Look, listen, and feel for air exchange. If no breath is present begin rescue breathing (i.e., CPR).

▷ **Circulation** - Check for gross external bleeding, and take these actions to control bleeding if necessary:

- Apply direct pressure with bandage to area bleeding.

- Use elevation (unless an extremity is fractured).

- Use pressure points.
  - ▷ Use the Carotid Artery located in the groove felt between the Adams Apple and the neck muscle, on either side of the neck.
  - ▷ Use the Brachial Artery located on the inside of the upper arm between the biceps and triceps muscle.
  - ▷ Use the Femoral Artery located in the upper, inner aspect of the thigh or groin area.
    - Apply a Tourniquet as a last resort to control bleeding. Failure to control bleeding will definitely lead to death. Place the tourniquet two inches above the wound and ensure the material utilized is at least two inches wide. Put a "T" on the victim's forehead to include the time and date the tourniquet was applied. Seek medical response immediately!

▶ Check and treat for shock.

▷ Control all obvious external bleeding.

▷ Treat all wounds (i.e., cover with dressing and bandage).

▷ Splint any possible fractures or trauma to extremities.

▷ Give nothing by mouth—not even water.

▷ Elevate legs 6-12 inches unless leg fracture, chest injury, or isolated head injury.

▷ Cover victim on top and bottom to keep warm.

▷ Transport victim for formal medical treatment.

▶ Treat all wounds:

▷ Wounds: Cover with dressing and bandage.

▷ Open Chest Wounds: Cover wound with victims credit card or equivalent. Have victim exhale and tape card down on three sides and lay the victim on injured side.

▷ Open Abdominal Wounds: Gather intestines still connected; place intestines on the abdomen, but not back inside the wound; avoid any pressure to the abdomen; cover wound with moist dressing; flex the persons knees; and give nothing by mouth—not even water.

▷ Fractures: Apply the splint so it extends to the joints above and below the suspected fracture sight. Always splint fractures in the position found unless there is no distal pulse. **NOTE:** If no pulse, reposition with slight traction until a pulse is felt.

▷ Traumatic Amputations (example: arm blown or cut off): Apply a tourniquet to the stump. Ensure that the tourniquet is not less than two inches in width and is placed no more than two inches above the amputated section. Put a "T" on the victim's forehead to include the time and date the tourniquet was applied.

▷ Impaled Objects: Stabilize the object with a bulky dressing and try to reduce the size of the object. Do not pull the object out (example: Attempting to pull a knife out of the stomach).

NOTE: As a positive outcome of the Iraq war, the medical establishment has developed a quick blood clot solution that will stop bleeding immediately. This solution should not be used before the use of the tourniquet if a victim can quickly be taken to a hospital, and it still must be used as a last resort! This is important because the solution may stop bleeding, but may cause other damages to body tissue. So, use this modern blood clot solution (if you have access to it) only if it will take prolonged time to get the victim to the hospital and you know continued rapid bleeding will surely result in death. Moreover, this blood clot solution may only be available to military combat units.

SPECIAL NOTE: Each checklist was created as a stand-alone guide. Therefore information contained in one checklist may be contained in another.

CHECKLIST 21
Gangs Informational Checklist

According to **Carl S. Taylor** (Michigan State University), author of **"Dangerous Society,"** gangs can be categorized into three groups **(i.e., Scavengers, Territorials, and Corporate). Scavenger gangs** are normally illiterate people who are prone to violent erratic behavior, and just want to belong to a group. Leaders change often and members are normally (not always) from urban environments and their crimes are characterized as petty, senseless, and opportunistic. **Territorial gangs** employ violent confrontation to protect perceived turf and defend their business or enterprise. They may attempt to establish leadership roles in communities and *members* are protected from predatory gangs. Plus, their "territorial law" is dominant over "traditional law". **Corporate gangs** are the most organized state gangs, and they are well organized with strong leaders and managers. Their membership is based on a person's worth or contribution to the gang, and discipline is highly structured and ruthlessly enforced. Their criminal activity is motivated solely for profit, and leadership attempts to develop a semblance of legitimacy by channeling illegal profits into legitimate business enterprises. *They will even seek political leverage!* **NOTE:** Areas of high unemployment, heavy welfare concentration, poor schools, and deteriorating neighborhoods (e.g., cause behind Criminal Justice Broken Windows Theory) are seen as the breeding ground for gang activity (but definitely not all)!

You should know there are hundreds of different

street gangs in the United States and all over the world. All nations and cultures have people who have chosen this path in life; so, I will just name a few. You should contact your local law enforcement officials to gain knowledge of what gangs exist in your community. You should also remember that most street gangs exist to obtain financial gain just like the American Mafia's, and others gangs may be formed and motivated primarily by hate. It really does not matter what causes a gang to form. What really matters is that you could become their next victim either intentionally or by accident. Find out what gangs are present in your community, stay away from them, and report gang activity to law enforcement officials.

Some Common Gangs:

► Bloods (various groups throughout country)

► Crips (various groups throughout country)

► Gangster Disciples

► The Rolling 20's

► Latin Kingz

► F.O.L.KS

► Insane Spanish Cobras

► Maniac Latin Disciples

► Cash Flow Posse

► Vice Lords

► Hells Angels

► Blood Brothers International

► Chinese Tongs

► Hip Sing

► Wah Ching

► Wo Hop To Triad

► Local Boys

► Black Widows

► Wolf Boys

► Yakuza

► Vietnamese BTK

► Italian Mafia

► Cuban Mafia

► Mexican Mafia

► Jamaican Mafia

► Russian Mafia

► Various hate and militia organizations, etc.

Note that this list can be expanded in great detail; but on a positive note, it must be brought to light that some of the above groups are changing their evil ways and are displaying more positive behavior. However, to proactively manage risk in your lives consider using the internet to research gangs in your area. In fact, research some of the internet sites and books outlined below or at Checklist 28 to enhance your mental data base; yet, please note that web sites change all the time, so some may not open. If not, just use your search engine and search for the required document by name.

Key Internet Sites and Books:

▶ **http://members.aol.com/ggarner539/** - This site is called the Garner Gang Home Page and contains information on just about every gang or hate group in the US. This is a great place to start research.

▶ **http://www.splcenteer.org/** - This is the Southern Poverty Law Center (SPLC) home page. This is also a great source of information on hate groups. Communicates hate groups locations and recent incidents.

▶ **An Introduction to Gangs** written by George Knox.

▶ **Street Gang Awareness: A Resource for Parents and Professionals** written by Steven Sachs.

▶ **Monster** written by Kody Scott.

▶ **Gathering Storm: Americas Militia Threat** written by Morris Dees.

▶ **8 Ball Chicks: A Year in the Violent World of Girl Gang Members** written by Gini Sikes.

▶ **Gangs: A Handbook for Community Awareness** written by Rick Landre, Mike Miller and Dee Porter.

▶ **Skinhead Street Gangs** written by Loren Christensen.

▶ **Born Fi Dead; A Journey through the Jamaican Posse Underground** written by Laurie Gunst.

▶ **Understanding Street Gangs** written by Wes McBride and Robert Jackson.

NOTE: This list can be very extensive. Gaining knowledge of groups located in your community will enhance family and/or personal safety.

SPECIAL NOTE: *Each checklist was created as a stand-alone guide. Therefore information contained in one checklist may be contained in another.*

CHECKLIST 22
Names of Suspected Hate Groups Checklist

Use this checklist to identify yourself with names of hate groups who are suspected of evil acts, and in many cases are officially documented to have committed acts of domestic terrorism against minorities, other citizens, and government employees and facilities for decades. If you want to increase your knowledge base, review the Southern Poverty Law Center's (SPLC) internet web page where you will find and extensive list of groups under the Hate Group Intelligence section.

Potential Hate Groups:

▶ Ku Klux Klan (KKK): Was founded in Pulaski, Tennessee, and has been around since the reconstruction era (after the civil war). Members are located in just about every city and state in America, and are responsible for countless murders of African Americans, other minorities, and other citizens since their existence. In addition, the KKK backed countless people elected as state and federal Senators and Congressmen over the decades as openly communicated on television by the History Channel. Securing the vote for these people enabled the legislation of laws that kept minorities or subordinated cultures in their so-called place for centuries. Conversely, President Barack Obama recorded in his book titled "The Audacity of Hope" that Senator Robert C. Byrd of West Virginia received his first taste of leadership in his early twenties as a member of the Raleigh County Ku Klux Klan, and he became a US Senator.

▶ Aryan Nations: Founded in 1974 by Richard Girnt Butler and is headquartered in Idaho. Acts as an umbrella organization for other supremacist like-minded organizations, and consist of many other groups with slightly different names.

▶ Patriot Movement: A diverse grouping or network of Christian right-wingers, white supremacist, and anti-federal government protesters. One of many examples would be the Arizona Patriots.

▶ Militia Groups: According to Bruce Hoffman, author of Inside Terrorism, over 800 militia groups are dispersed throughout every state in America. Most claim to be Patriots (indicated above), but not all Patriots have joined a militia. Militia groups are associated in the public perception with two beliefs: White supremacy and opposition to "Big" government. Militia organizers claim they have at least five million members throughout the United States. The more prominent militias are the Militia of Montana, North American Volunteer Militia, Big Star One, Texas Constitutional Militia, West Virginia Mountaineer Militia, and the Michigan Militia.

▶ The Order: Another neo-militia organization associated with the Aryan Nations.

▶ Skin Heads: Another neo-Nazi hate group led by Tom and John Metzgar. Responsible for hundreds of murders and assaults on minorities. Identified by their shaven heads. As they grow older, they regrow hair and assimilate into the dominant culture maintaining and reinforcing hate group ideology. **NOTE:** Since Russia became a capitalist state and allowed immigration, many young Russians blaming unemployment and economic hardship on minorities *instead of improving themselves* have developed their own Neo Nazi organizations that have assaulted and sometimes murdered innocent immigrants. This hate is not hard to understand because of perceived competition associated with access to money (and/or descent salary jobs) and access to the best mates, but it is difficult to understand how such organizations could gain power in Russia where NAZI's led by Hitler killed thousands to millions of Russians during World War II.

▶ Conservative Citizens Council (CCC): A modern group composed of primarily right-wing, wealthy, educated, European-American, Christian (usually... non-Catholic) heterosexual males who represent a backlash against the effects of the liberalization of US politics and society during the 1960's and 1970's. Basically, this group shares a similar ideology to that of the KKK and Aryan Nations. For those who watch CSPAN, you may be able to catch one of their conferences. Watching their conferences becomes important if you want to learn their angle to changing America—that is, in a more negative way for minorities or subordinated cultures.

▶ National Organization of European American Rights (NOFEAR): A new group led by Ku Klux Klansman and Louisiana State Legislator David Duke. Group generally composed of the same group of people who are members of the CCC.

▶ The Nation of Islam: Led by The Minister Louis Farrakhan and headquartered in Chicago, Illinois. The reason I added this group to the list is that many Americans see this group as a hate group bent on destruction of the European-American culture. As an American Christian who studies such groups for the protection and benefit of others, I do not believe this label is completely true. In fact, Muslims are God fearing people who are taught to love their fellow man just like Christians are supposed to do; yet, key emphasis is put on who is perceived as a "fellow-man". This specific Muslim group has grown up in America having to deal with the overwhelming negative traits of our countries past and present. However, in my 49+ years of life, I am yet to read a story about a Nation of Islam member or group initiating a physical assault on any American citizen other than **Malcolm X.** *Yet, such an act of violence has more than likely overtly/covertly occurred because of violent human nature, and maybe by a few other groups like the New Black Panther Party, some common street gang, or hateful people.* Moreover, although there exit members who have delivered hate filled speeches, many scholars believe this negative dialog comes in response to perceived acts of racism. ***But, as wise people know—two wrongs can never make a right!*** However, when confronted with violence, these Americans will defend themselves just like most other Americans—either through litigation or through physical force as seen in America's response to 9/11. **Key Note To Remember:** There are over 800 anti-minority hate groups in America alone, and only one Nation of Islam! *Yet, in order to start building a better America or protecting innocent people from hate crimes,* **national leaders** *must strive to build stronger partnerships among citizens in effort to construct a more positive present and future.*

▶ The New Black Panther Party: Seen by many terrorist experts from different cultures as a Black or African American hate group whose ideology is the separation of the white and black so-called races/cultures. Of course, my personal belief is that this is the type of group some African Americans join who are angry with our political system, which has for centuries mistreated them; therefore, these people see no positive solution other than complete separation of the races/cultures. In addition, members may join such organizations, because they feel this is the only way to protect themselves from violence and/or unfair imprisonment. Of course, due to the struggle for perceived scarce resources (i.e., the struggle for money/jobs and designated members of the opposite sex, etc.) this goal may never fully occur. *Additionally, I personally believe there are more descent people in the world than bad who just want to live in peace and harmony with other Earthlings correctly called "The Human Race" (i.e., the only race, in my humble opinion)!*

▶ **The Targets and the Perpetrators:** The potential targets for hate group protest or violent action are varied as reflected in their target selections (e.g., tax offices, federal agency employees, abortion clinics, and subordinated cultures, etc). However, concerned citizens should realize hate group organizations are not all uneducated southern people, but are also well educated citizens coming from every segment of society. Many are even professionally trained to conduct terrorist operations as openly boasted by hate group leaders themselves.

NOTE: This list can be expanded in great detail. Remember, these groups are also supported by money contributing sympathizers who are so abundant they cannot be adequately counted. Please review the Southern Poverty Law Center's (SPLC) internet web page to determine hate groups located in your city. The list is growing!

*Conversely, after having read this data, a fascinated person may ask, **"Why all the hate?"**, but many people have probably heard this statement from some older gentlemen or woman who has been in the America for four or more decades, and that statement is normally, **"Son, money & women make the world go round."** Now, you may say, **"What barring does this have on the subject?"** Well, in my experienced and educated opinion as an African American male, I will answer this question in this way. For those of you who have taken an intro-level Sociology course, you know that less than 10% of Americans control over 90% of US monetary resources; therefore, the remaining 90% of the population must find some way to obtain the life sustaining remaining 10%. Therefore, since the dominant culture in America basically led in development of the United States; many Americans (not all) that fall in this category assume they have a special right to these remaining funds. Plus, leaders require votes to stay in power in effort to continue receiving a substantial government salary and an awesome retirement check each month for the remainder of their lives* *(i.e., enjoyment of what the American Pageant history book called the government spoils system). So, for those citizens in pursuit of the remaining 10% of resources, extreme levels of competition is played out by these humans where they compete for the two most precious resources (i.e., access to money/jobs and the best mates). Yes, money makes the modern world go around, but you must obtain a quality job in order to obtain money. In order to obtain a quality job, a worker must be educated in a given task and/or profession (e.g., jobs equate to money). This is why for decades subordinated cultures received no formal education or the worst formal education in America, and countless scientific lies were used to justify this system when the true cause was hate-based competition for perceived scarce resources. Now, when it comes down to obtaining desired mates the Christian bible and the Torah communicates Adam resided in the Garden of Eden and had everything, yet was not happy. Therefore, the Creator did not give him a Chrysler 300, Mercedes, Cadillac, BMW, Honda Civic, Suzuki XL-7, or drugs—which probably grew naturally all around him. No, the Creator gave him Eve (a woman). Adam loved this woman so much that he decided to listen to Eve over the Creator. This is how important WOMAN is to a heterosexual MAN (and visa-versa), and competitive access to the best mate has led to all kinds of unfair actions (or evils).*

Well, in America all cultures of humans have mated with one another since the first arrival of Europeans and Africans in the 1500's-1600's, but the leading class of Americans formulated laws that prohibited these love connections which directly resulted in less competition for the women they perceived to be theirs.

So, there you have it. The root cause of most everything hateful in America is the historic competition played out over the two most important resources to modern MAN and WOMAN, and those resources are jobs which equates to money, and control over specific members of the opposite sex! Moreover, abundant access to money/jobs will provide easier access to the desired mates!

Finally, in 2011 we live in a world where the door to equality is more open than in the past, and is changing former rules and many people from the dominate culture, and some from the subordinate culture do not like these changes at all (e.g., those decently employed female members of the minority community who get upset when they see a descent minority male now dating a member of the dominate culture, and even though their basic needs are satisfied via quality employment, they still feel they must compete for what they perceive is theirs—that strong minority male. One can see this mentality displayed even when the employed female already has their very own mate of choice).

Personally, I look forward to an America where all of its citizens are educated and prepared to tackle "Globalization" head own. I also look forward to seeing millions of the beautiful and strong offspring that people from different cultures create. It will simply work to make the world a more beautiful and happier place!

Yet, good people must keep their eyes open at all times, because millions of people do not like this vision and see it as a loss of control and become fearful and extremely dangerous!

SPECIAL NOTE: *Each checklist was created as a stand-alone guide. Therefore information contained in one checklist may be contained in another.*

CHECKLIST 23
Names of Suspected Anti-Minority Churches Checklist

Utilize this checklist to familiarize yourself with hate-based churches. In order to gain knowledge of other churches not on the list below, please review the SPLC web page. Additionally, this information should not come as a surprise you, but renowned terrorist expert Mr. Bruce Hoffman outlined in his book called "Inside Terrorism" that religion has become the primary motivation for terrorism as seen vividly in the Middle East. Moreover, many people will ask why (?), but just think about it for a minute. When was the last time some heavenly angel appeared before a congregation and openly communicated to some charismatic religious leader that they grossly misinterpreted the scripter? Well, the answer to this question in *real life* is **"never"**. Therefore, if you say the Creator stands behind some community ideology, and especially to a group of people who pay to hear this message; then these people born with the gift of gab can rest assure they will not be publicly corrected! So there you have it, religion can be a great motivational tool to get across certain messages (both good and evil)!

NOTE: Even the Hebrews communicated in the Torah (and also in the Bible) that the Creator told them to enter into a new land (called the Promised Land) and kill all inhabitants (i.e., men, and women who had known men, or precisely, those who had slept with men—a good idea since sexually transmitted diseases were probably just as prevalent during those times as they are today).

This is the basic reason so much hate has existed in this region over the centuries—people are basically seeking revenge, and now the situation is similar to street gang violence in America, only on a far worst level of violence. I personally call it "Gang Banging on a National Level", which is primarily based on hate and revenge!

Some of the Churches are indicated below:

▶ **The World Church of the Creator:** Led by Mr. Matt Hale and has spread churches throughout the United States.

▶ **Christian Identity:** European Americans who believe they are the lost tribes of Israel (Original Hebrews) and believe America is the Promised Land. If you have knowledge of the Bible, then you know the creator supposedly told the original Hebrews to destroy all other inhabitants of the Promised Land (i.e., what is now Israel; yet, America for these believers). Well, under the Christian Identity belief this means all non-white Americans must die, be banished, or be placed in servitude (i.e., prison/jail). Additionally, renowned terrorist expert Mr. Bruce Hoffman also indicated in his book "Inside Terrorism [1998]" that the basic tenants of the contemporary American version of the Identity Movement includes the beliefs; that:

▷ Jesus Christ was not a Semite, but an Aryan
▷ The lost tribes of Israel are composed *not of Jews*, but of "blue-eyed" Aryans
▷ That white Anglo-Saxons and not Jews are the true "Chosen People"
▷ That the United States is the "Promised Land"

▷ That Jews are viewed as impostors and children of Satan who must be exterminated

   ▸ **NOTE:** *Some Americans may ask, "How could something like this happen?" Well, the truth is; all it takes is a charismatic leader blessed with the gift of gab who can tell people a story they want to believe and are willing to pay ten percent or more of their earnings to hear. These leaders can do this in complete faith that they will not be punished on Earth, because when was the last time any so called Profit received a visit from God scolding him/her for their negative communications. The answer is simply—* **NEVER***; and this should be easily understood by Christians who believe Godly punishment is reserved for Judgment Day! In other words, there may be a Heavenly date all these people must meet; and if "Karma" is true, and people are hurt due to their crime-oriented motivational communications, they may surely pay a debt while on Earth as well. At least, that seems to be what I have observed in my time on Earth!*

▷ That Christian Identity churches are numerous, and a few Christian Identity churches are indicated below (See SPLC web page for the complete and updated list):

   ▸ *Keys to the Kingdom Church in St. Augustine, FL.*

   ▸ *Ministry of Christ Church in Mariposa, CA.*

   ▸ *Remnant of Israel in Opportunity, WA.*

   ▸ *Sacred Truth Ministries in Mountain City, TN.*

   ▸ *Revelation Books in Staunton, VA.*

- *Virginia Christian Israelites in Round Hill, VA.*

- *Old Order Israelite Brethren in Mountain View, AR.*

- *Scriptures for America's Ministries in LPorte, CO.*

- *Shepherd's Chapel in Sebring, FL*

- **NOTE:** *This list could consume this page and the next. This type of ideology is deeply ingrained in American society. Therefore, nothing you see racist in America should come as a shock to any knowledgeable person. People who swear up and down that our country does not have serious race or cultural hate problems are either: (1) ignorant, (2) uninformed, (3) living in a military area (mandatory goodwill practiced Utopias), or are (4) Legals or Insiders hiding in the system doing the work of their brethren until they can safely come out of the closet.*

► **The Nation of Islam:** See Checklist 22.

► **Christian Patriot Movement**: According to Bruce Hoffman the aims and motivations of this extremist movement is to spread a broad spectrum of anti-federalist and seditious beliefs coupled with religious hatred and racial intolerance, masked by a transparent veneer of religious precepts. They are bound together by an ethos which includes these beliefs:

  ▷ Hostility to any form of government above the country level (i.e., anti-United Nations ideology)

▷ The vilification of Jews and non-whites as children of Satan

▷ An obsession with achieving the religious and racial purification of the United States

▷ Belief in a conspiracy theory of powerful Jewish interest controlling the government and the media

▷ Advocacy of the overthrow of the US government, or the Zionist Occupation Government (ZOG) as Patriot/Militia groups disparagingly refer to it.

SPECIAL NOTE: *Each checklist was created as a stand-alone guide. Therefore information contained in one checklist may be contained in another.*

CHECKLIST 24
Dates Suspected Hate Groups
May Attack Checklist

Utilize this checklist to familiarize yourself with the dates domestic hate groups, extremist/terrorist groups, and/or mentally deranged people may attack the general population. It will be wise to take personal interest in your safety on the anniversary dates of critical incidents outlined below, and especially if hateful events have taken place in your specific community. Keep in mind, as more crimes occur, new dates may be added to this list. One of these dates could be April 16, 2007—the day a mentally deranged person killed over 30 people at Virginia Tech University.

Dates of Attack:

► **01 Jan: US:** Any New Year's Celebration!

► **26 Feb: US:** Anniversary World Trade Center bombing in NY

► **28 Feb: US:** Anniversary of initial engagement on the Branch Davidian compound in Waco, Texas by ATF in 1993

► **19 Apr: US:** Anniversary of the ATF & FBI **Waco, Texas** Branch Davidian compound siege, and also the anniversary of 1995 **Alfred P. Murrah** Federal Building in Oklahoma City bombing, where 168 people were killed and over 500 injured. The government later determined Timothy MVeigh was guilty of committing the crime, and was suspected of being associated with the Michigan Militia.

▶ **28 Apr: US:** The day Richard Baumhammers, 34, a lawyer from Mount Lebanon, Pennsylvania opened fire in suburban Pittsburgh killing five minorities (one Indian, two Asians, one Jew, and an African American). This was most likely in response to another shooting in that region where an African American man named Ronald Taylor allegedly shouted racial epithets before fatally shooting three European American males. This will most likely become a common scenario that is witnessed by many in the near future unless **national leaders** take essential steps to positively **change** many hateful ideologies that work against a *positive and team-oriented* American evolution.

▶ **3 Jul: Iran/US:** USS Vincennes downed Iran Air Flight 655, killing 290 people on board (1998).

▶ **4 Jul: US:** Independence Day (1776)—the holiday weekend Benjamin Smith of Illinois went on a weekend shooting spree killing two minorities and injuring nine others. He was suspected of being a member the World Church of the Creator (a white supremacist church) which is led by Mr. Matt Hale.

▶ **10 Jul: Saudi Arabia:** Explosions at the holy mosque in Mecca killing 17 pilgrims (1989).

▶ **9 Sep: US:** The day the Twin Towers and a portion of the Pentagon were supposedly destroyed by two airline jets that were seized by terrorist.

▶ **Sep: US/Africa:** Embassy bombing in Africa (Nairobi, Kenya and Dar es Salaam, Tanzania).

▶ **20 Oct: US:** Atlanta, GA Olympic Games bombing. Mr. Eric Rudolph is accused of conducting that terrorist act and is also suspected of bombing an abortion clinic in Alabama.

▶ **23 Oct: US:** Gynecologist (abortion doctor) assassinated by sniper in Buffalo, NY. Murder was suspected of being linked to the Army of God—an extreme anti-government group.

NOTE: Many dates could be added to this list; yet, if you can think of any other noteworthy dates, then perhaps you should add them to this list and take the appropriate actions to protect yourself. Moreover, consider contacting your local law enforcement authorities for assistance in gathering current threat information.

SPECIAL NOTE: *Each checklist was created as a stand-alone guide. Therefore information contained in one checklist may be contained in another.*

CHECKLIST 25
Bomb Threat Checklist

Hopefully, you may never be the recipient of a telephonic bomb threat; but if you are, please consider using the following procedures to record the threat. Additionally, a copy of this list should be placed by phones in the office or home and family members should be instructed on proper use. **NOTE:** Bomb threats are made all the time, and may be a hoax or real; however, this risk must be appropriately managed. Perhaps this data would have been useful during the 1960's when citizens were fighting for equal rights and routinely received telephonic bomb threats.

Actions/Tips:

▶ Record the local number at which *call is received,* and record the caller's telephone number if visible on your telephone's redial screen.

▶ Record (or remember) the length of the call:

▶ Record (or remember) time and the date of call:

▶ Record (or remember) the exact wording of the threat received:

▶ Ask the following questions while the caller is still on the telephone line:
  ▷ When is the bomb going to explode?
  ▷ Where is it right now?
  ▷ What does it look like?
  ▷ What kind of bomb is it?

▷ What will cause it to explode?

▷ Did you personally place the bomb?

▷ Why?

▷ Where are you?

▷ What is your name?

▶ Gain as much information as possible and then leave the telephone off the hook and call the police immediately.

▶ Authorities may require additional information from you. Please strive to remember the following characteristics about the caller:

▷ Caller's sex, age, accent.

▷ Background sounds: Streets, Airplanes, Voices, Music, etc.

▷ Language type: Educated, Foul, Irrational, Taped Message etc.

SPECIAL NOTE: *Each checklist was created as a stand-alone guide. Therefore information contained in one checklist may be contained in another.*

CHECKLIST 26
Handling Suspicious Biological/ Chemical Weapons Delivered Packages Checklist

Within the United States there have been several threats to use biological or chemical (BIO/CHEM) weapons on the general populace by domestic and foreign terrorist or crazies. Most have been hoaxes, but a few critical incidents have occurred; however, some of these BIO/CHEM incidents may go unnoticed for some period of time due to late detection. In fact, many suspicious packages have been mailed to organizations and individuals; yet, people should know what steps to take to neutralize such incidents. Therefore, consider reviewing the SCENARIO checklist below to assist you in effectively handling suspicious packages mailed to your home or work center that could potentially enclose BIO/ CHEM weapons as witnessed in the Washington D.C. "anthrax critical incident" a short time after 9/11.

Action/Tips:

SCENARIO: An administrator, a secretary, or an addressee opens an envelope and finds a message implying the envelope contains Anthrax (or some other chemical/biological material) and that the person has become contaminated. **(Try to remember the exact words used. It will be important during the first responder assessment phase.)**

► If you are the person who removed the letter or note from the envelope, leave it out and gently place the letter and the envelope back on the surface of the desk, tabletop credenza, etc.

▶ Inform coworkers in you immediate office area, but do not allow anyone to touch or approach the letter or envelope. Account for everyone in the immediate area by full name, office assignment, etc. If possible, prevent further circulation of material by turning off fans/ventilation systems. Then close off/lock the office and have everyone exit to another unoccupied office. **NOTE:** If you suspect a person has been contaminated, do not allow them to leave the room unless emergency first responders approve this decision. Allowing these people to leave may potentially spread the hazard!

▶ Once in the other office, immediately notify building security personnel and law enforcement personnel.

▶ Inform security or law enforcement officials of the exact contents and characteristics of the note (i.e., the type, the color, size of the envelope, addressee, postmark, marks on the envelope, and description of any contents found within or on the note). **(Do not re-approach the envelope or letter to gather the above information, once the room has been cleared).**

▶ Also tell the police authority the approximate date and time you received the envelope and by what delivery system (FEDEX, UPS, courier, etc.).

▶ **REMEMBER:** It is very important the person relating the information regarding the letter does not "paraphrase" the threat when forwarding it to law enforcement authorities. As mentioned above, remember the exact wording of the document and state the message verbatim to the security or law enforcement authority. When police have the exact wording of the letter then assessment of the threat can be expedited.

▶ **FINAL NOTE TO REMEMBER:** For telephonic threats, use Checklist 26 that covers bomb threats and follow the above listed procedures for notification.

NOTE 1: Rest assure law enforcement personnel are actively attempting to neutralize CHEM/BIO threats as you read this document. But citizens should know it is only a matter of time before a large incident like the one that occurred on Japan's subway system **(i.e., the release of Sarin Nerve Gas by an Anti-government group)** occurs in America. As a matter of fact Mr. Bruce Hoffman in his book called "Inside Terrorism[1998]" indicated that in 1984 a non-lethal, but disturbingly portentous incident occurred in the small Oregon town of Dalles, where followers of the Bhagwan Shree Rajneesh poisoned the local reservoir and contaminated the salad-bars of restaurants with salmonella bacteria in hopes of debilitating the local populace and thereby rigging a key municipal election in the cult's favor. It should be noted that this charismatic ascetic Indian mystic had many wealthy donators since he had amassed a collection of 93 Rolls-Royce automobiles.

Moreover as biological, nuclear, and chemical technology and materials reaches the common man, we can expect the use of these materials to prove some ideological point in the near future.

NOTE 2: In the military they call materials like Sarin Gas (i.e., chemical weapon), Anthrax (i.e., biological weapon), and nuclear bombs—Weapons of Mass Destruction (WMD). Remember this acronym, because it will be used in a great number of conversations.

SPECIAL NOTE: Each checklist was created as a stand-alone guide. Therefore information contained in one checklist may be contained in another.

CHECKLIST 27
Church Security Enhancement Checklist

I highly recommend ministers, priest, and preachers consider taking the steps indicated in the checklist below to enhance security of their designated prayer facilities. In recent times' vandalism, larceny, and theft at churches, mosques, and cathedrals have increased tremendously. This type of activity is primarily motivated by hate and financial gain and is not expected to subside anytime in the near future. Although prayer is an excellent step to take, religious leadership should take the appropriate steps to harden (i.e., make more secure) their facilities. Hardening your facility may lead potential criminals to other softer (i.e., non-secure) targets. Inevitably, this will save your organization money, personal hardship, and grief.

Actions/Tips:

▶ Recommend contacting a security firm to help you harden your facility. If security professionals are already members of your church, then ministers should solicit their support.

▶ Install a security system similar to those installed at homes that annunciate (i.e., receive alarms) at the local police station or security service.

▶ Consider contacting a security service to periodically check your facility.

▶ If a security service is too expensive, consider task-ing and scheduling church members to periodically check out the facility. If it is impossible to routinely manage this task, consider conducting the task only during increased tensions (i.e., recent/nearby church burning incidents, recently passed equal opportunity legislation, or when hate group organizations have communicated threats).

▶ Install close circuit television (CCTV) surveillance at your facility with an image recording device. If this is too expensive, consider purchasing simulated (fake) video cameras and erecting them in places where they can be observed. Although this will not record activities, it will deter unknowledgeable criminals who suspect the CCTV system is operational. *Note that many electronic equipment merchants may be able to assist you.*

▶ Consider having someone monitor entry into the church during sessions. This will aid in assessment of hostile acts early enough to give church members time to take appropriate emergency actions and deter potential trouble makers.

NOTE: If any of these procedures had been implemented in the past, it may have prevented the 1999 church shootings in Texas and California, and the Church burnings in Alabama and Mississippi that occurred between 2004 and 2006.

▶ Consider having the police monitor major meetings where there is a possibility hostilities may occur or hire a quality security firm.

▶ When a hostile threat has been communicated, consider having the police search and clear facilities for explosives. This task should be conducted for certain; even if your organization has not taken steps to harden its complex.

▶ Finally, church explosions and/or fires caused by arsonist have taken place for centuries right here in America and throughout the world. *Human hate and complete ignorance is the primary cause of such atrocities, but the hate is predominately motivated by the competition over two perceived scarce resources (i.e.., money [made via jobs] and attainment of the desired mate).* Either ministers take steps to secure their places of worship or suffer the consequences. Please realize, some hate group member may be planning to set your church on fire right now! *Evil is—what Evil does; and because of this fact, I often wonder if God's former number #1 Angel (i.e., Lucifer or Satan by name) was removed from Heaven and incarcerated on Earth; then why are we humans in the same place? Moreover, if Earth is a prison; then, I guess citizens should better understand the evil that goes on each and every day. I just do not understand why good and/or descent loving humans are on Earth sharing space with evil and extremely dangerous people.* However, this will be one of my questions on judgment day; yet, until that day comes, please take serious efforts to evaluate the local threat to your church and take required protective actions.

SPECIAL NOTE: *Each checklist was created as a stand-alone guide. Therefore information contained in one checklist may be contained in another.*

CHECKLIST 28
Books You Should Read Checklist

Information is power, and in modern times there are several dynamic books written by distinguished professionals to enhance the knowledge of common citizens and foreigners. In fact, books outlined below are phenomenal in that they provide knowledge often times not found in the home or church that will enlighten readers and enhance their understanding of our societal **threats or risks** we all face in today's world. Therefore, if you can find the time, I recommend reading the following books to build knowledge and skills.

Protection Oriented Books To Read:

▶ **The Turner Diaries:** Written by William Pierce under the pseudonym Andrew MaDonald. This book is not found in stores, but can be found at almost any gun show in the United States. It basically outlines the planned takeover of America by anti-American organizations. Remember the proceeds of this book may go towards the growth of hate groups. *A must read!*

▶ **Jane's World Insurgency and Terrorism Book:** Written by Jane's Information Group and talks about historic and modern terrorist groups, and is also found on the internet. *A must read!*

▶ **Harden the Target:** Written by Thomas Adams.

Gives further guidance on protecting your home, self, and family. ***A must read!***

▶ **JET Magazine:** Published by the Johnson Publishing Company. All Americans, but especially African and Latino Americans should read JET Magazine routinely. It provides minorities with information they might not find elsewhere.

▶ **The Coming Race War in America**: Written by Carl T. Rowan. Gives hypothetical dialog about a potential race or culture war in America. ***A must read!***

▶ **The Isis Papers "The Keys To The Colors":** Written by Dr. Frances Cress Welsing and talks about issues associated with dominating versus subordinated cultures. ***A must read!***

▶ **Emerging Viruses:** AIDS & Ebola, "Nature, Accident, or Intentional?" Reference Edition: Written by Leonard G. Horowitz, D.M.D., M.A., M.P.H. ***A must read—very critical!***

▶ **BIOHAZARDS**: Written by Ken Alibek with Stephen Handelman. Outlines the life of a former Soviet Union military scientist who manufactured biological weapons for the state. This book is a great follow-up to Emerging Viruses. ***A must read.***

▶ **The Holy Bible,** *"Original African Heritage Edition"* King James Version: Published by the James C. Winston Publishing Company and edited by The Reverend Cain Hope Felder, Ph.D. The bible gives a historic breakdown of the scriptures from a viewpoint not often taught in America. Knowledge will help you better understand what is going on in the world today and enhance your ability to protect yourself. I recommend you start with Proverbs since there are 31 Proverbs (i.e., one for each day)—King Solomon's book! *A must read.*

▶ **Terrorism, Asymmetric Warfare, and Weapons of Mass Destruction:** Written by Anthony Cordesman [2002], and talks about the world wide use of biological, chemical and radioactive weapons by many players. *A must read!*

▶ **The New Face of Terrorism:** Written by Nadine Gurr and Benjamin Cole, and talks about the world wide use of biological, chemical and radioactive weapons. *A must read!*

▶ **America's Achilles' Heel:** Written by Richard Falkenrath, Robert Newman, and Bradley Thayer, and it talks biological, chemical, nuclear, and radio-active detonated devices, and how they may affect the world in the near future. *A must read!*

▶ **Inside Terrorism:** Written by Bruce Hoffman a world renowned terrorist expert who communicates in-depth knowledge on both domestic and foreign terrorist groups and their potential motivations. *A must read!*

▶ **Countering the New Terrorism:** Written by the RAND Corporation and talks about modern terrorist trends and the modern concept called **"NETWAR"**, which deals directly with the networking of terrorist and/or criminal organizations all over the world just like the western allied nations. *A must read!*

▶ **Origins of Terrorism--Psychologies, Ideologies,**

Theologies, States of Mind: Written by Walter Reich and deals with the psychological and religious motivations for terrorist acts and gives some great ideas on how to effectively address terrorist problems. *A must read!*

► **Terrorism Handbook--For Operational Responders, 1st or 2nd Edition:** Written by Armando Bevelacqua and talks about some of the known biological, chemical and radio-active weapons, and how first responders must prepare and effectively respond to the use of these weapons of mass destruction by terrorist and/or criminals.

► **Contemporary Security Management:** Written by John J. Fay and talks about steps security managers and people looking to enhance their personal or facility protection programs. This is an awesome security management text book—*a must read for Security Managers!*

► **Security and Loss Prevention:** Written by Paul Purpura and talks about steps security managers and people looking to enhance their personal or facility protection programs. This is an awesome security awareness text book—*a must read for Security Managers!*

► **Issues in Security Management--Thinking Critically About Security:** Written by Robert R. Robinson, and uses a series of security articles written by security experts to impart knowledge to security managers and people looking to enhance their personal or facility protection programs. This is an awesome security awareness text book—*a must read for Security Managers!*

▶ **Secrets:** Written by Rhonda Byrne where she talks about the universal law of attraction and how having a positive vision of the world can possibly attract positive occurrences in your life—*a dynamic must read!*

▶ **Come on People:** Written by Bill Cosby where he communicates problems in specific American culture that must be changed in order to improve individual lives in America—*a dynamic must read!*

▶ **Lies My Teacher Told Me:** Written by James W. Loewen that presents an enriching understanding of the US Education System, and provides deep insight into the true visions of many past leaders (both American and Foreign). *A dynamic must read novel that should be maintained on shelves at home.*

▶ **Risk Analysis and the Security Survey:** Written by James F. Broder, CPP that presents brilliant information on the successful conduct of Risk Management. *A dynamic must read novel that should be maintained on shelves at home.*

▶ **A People's History of the United States (1492 – Present):** Written by Howard Zinn that presents brilliant historical information on the evolution of the United States written from the perspective of those who were not in power. *A dynamic must read novel that should be maintained on shelves at home.*

▶ **Before the Mayflower, 6ᵗʰ Revised Edition.** Written by Lerone Bennett Jr. presents and enriching historic understanding of how Black and/or African Americans evolved alongside European Americans and other cultures within the United States. *A dynamic must read novel that should be maintained on shelves at home.*

▶ **Risk Analysis and Security Countermeasure Selection:** Written by Thomas Norman and effectively communicates how organizations can mitigate risk via thorough understanding of modern threats and the conduct of vulnerability assessments to counter these threats/risks. *A dynamic must read.*

SPECIAL NOTE: Each checklist was created as a stand-alone guide. Therefore information contained in one checklist may be contained in another.

CHECKLIST 29
Avoiding Modern Computer Crimes Checklist

Over the past years I have noticed many people who have fallen victim to modern computer crimes that did not exist in the late 1990's before computer technology and internet use became an advanced and common communications technique. The use of modern computer system communication tools (e.g., email and the internet) have caused politicians, religious leaders, police officers, military personnel, and many other professionals to experience embarrassing situations that have often led to reprimand or other criminal charges. Please realize that cyber crime has become as large as street crime, and law enforcement or government agencies at all levels have trained professionals to monitor internet and email traffic to decrease these crimes and identify potential criminals for prosecution. Plus, personal risk has been heightened by the enactment of the **United States Patriot Act** where many electronic communications can be screened in effort to mitigate terrorism and other criminal acts. Therefore, I believe it is critical young and older citizens properly utilize modern computer systems in effort to prevent computer crimes. Please consider using the checklist items listed below to help avoid these crimes.

Actions/Tips:

▶ Never participate in criminal activity!

▶ Never use computer and internet systems to participate in criminal activity!

► Realize that all computer systems or networks owned by federal or state facilities are subject to monitoring by competent computer system experts; therefore, all employees must take every step to ensure these computer systems are used for their intended purpose and nothing else!

► Realize that if a person is suspected of using their computer systems for internet crimes, all computers providing access to individuals under investigation (i.e., desk tops and/or lap tops) may be taken into custody as evidence. In addition, if a judge or U.S. Magistrate authorized the search of key facilities or objects where important evidence resides then information stored on your computer databases may also be taken as evidence. The key principle here is to always keep your activities legal!

► If communicating with superiors, peers, subordinates, and/or others over organizational computer systems is essential, consider taking these protective actions:

  ▷ Keep your communications professional. *Do not use organizational computers for pranks or jokes since the last laugh may be on you!*

  ▷ Never counsel subordinates via emails. Emails can be read over and over again an insight substantial anger in the email receiver which has led to many work place violence crimes motivated primarily by revenge. Therefore it is best to handle counseling situations face to face and professionally!

  ▷ Do not download any files on organizational

computers that might be illegal or be perceived as non-professional...**HOT!**

▷ Do not send personal emails on organizational computers when it is wiser to communicate the message via face-to-face communications, the phone, or via your own personal computer system...**HOT!**

▷ **Bottom Line:** Strive to keep computer communications professional because messages are subject to monitoring by employees, background check investigators, future employers, and/or potential mates...**HOT!**

SPECIAL NOTE: *Each checklist was created as a stand-alone guide. Therefore information contained in one checklist may be contained in another.*

CHECKLIST 30
Potential Actions the Government Can Take To Decrease Crime Checklist

It must be stated upfront that our elected leaders have all attempted to decrease some forms of crime, but have primarily used **fear** (e.g., imprisonment) to motivate stellar behavior in people and it is recorded by many psychologist and leadership professionals that fear cannot motivate consistent and positive change in humans. In fact, many criminals do not have *fear of being incarcerated* for their crimes because they do not plan on being **CAUGHT** and paying any restitution. Moreover, according to the Department of Justice the United States of America has an incarceration rate of 743 people per 100,000 of the national population (as of 2009)—*the highest in the world*. In comparison, Russia has the second highest 577 per 100,000, Canada is 123rd in the world with 117 per 100,000, and China has 120 per 100,000. *Additionally, during 2009 over 7.2 million people were at that time in* prison, *on* probation, *or on* parole. That means roughly 1 in every 32 Americans are held by the justice system. Also, according to the International Centre for Prison Studies (ICPS) at King's College London, of that 7.2 million, 2.3 million are in American prisons, and the People's Republic of China comes in second place with 1.6 million, despite its population being over *four times* that of the United States. So, while Americans only represent about 5 percent of the world's population, one-quarter of the entire world's inmates are incarcerated in the United States where some historians indicate less people were actually incarcerated in the now defunct Soviet Union. Moreover, security management and law enforcement expects have indicated for decades that the fear of punishment alone will not deter the majority of criminals. Especially, since getting **CAUGHT** for a crime is not something the typical criminal expects or even plans to happen! The truth is; true Crime Prevention in our nation can be improved substantially! In fact, taking crime prevention seriously (i.e., devising *proactive* crime prevention solutions) instead of depending predominately on after-the-act crime deterrence policies (i.e., *reactive* incarceration-oriented solutions) may work to better deter first time offenders from criminal activity. However, just like people have different size feet, humans will have different opinions; but, I honestly believe the recommendations highlighted below will work to significantly decrease crime in America and work to make our nation a more honorable society.

Actions/Tips:

► National leaders (i.e., Political, Criminal Justice System, Education, etc) at the federal and state levels must realize they cannot possibly know all the motivations/solutions to criminal activity, and especially since many of our national leaders have never resided in communities where street crimes occur and/or worked within the Wall Street economic system where multi-million dollar crimes routinely occur. Therefore, the motivation behind many crimes may not be known by people elected to govern the overall populace. So, it will be wise for our leaders to communicate with the populace that resides in high crime areas to talk about the potential root causes of crime. Now, it must be communicated that this conversation might not solely include mayors since it is a high possibility they do not reside in low income or high crime areas. It might be wise for national leaders to hold town meetings to talk directly with residents or seriously communicate with incarcerated criminals to determine the motivation behind their criminal acts. Once typical root causes of crimes are established, then root causes of crime can be effectively addressed via sound crime prevention programs aimed at reducing or eliminating crimes before they ever happen!

▶ National leaders must realize that conversations must be held with people perceived as enemies to society in effort to find out what motivates them (e.g., organized criminals, street criminals, hate groups, and potential or labeled terrorist organizations, etc). Failure to effectively communicate and gain an understanding into the mindset of these people or groups will hamper our ability to obtain knowledge that can be used to prevent others from participating in criminal activities. Additionally, these potential conversations may shed light on where national policies can be altered in effort to decrease hatred and poverty which motivates criminal activity.

▶ National leaders must make fair and just laws that apply equally to all citizens! I would honestly say we "missed the flight" on this principle as far as U.S. Drug Laws are written. *Yet, what do you think?*

Well, since I have never seen a perfect human on this planet, I believe we must use **Martin Luther King's** paraphrased advice on the establishment of laws as he outlined in his 1963 letter written while he was incarcerated in a Birmingham, Alabama prison calling for equal human rights:

> ▷ *... The answer lies in the fact that there are two types of laws: **just and unjust**.* I would be the first to advocate obeying just laws. One has not only a legal but a moral responsibility to obey just laws. Conversely, one has a moral responsibility to disobey unjust laws. I would agree with St. Augustine that *"an unjust law is no law at all."*....

> ▷ *...**Now, what is the difference between the two?*** How does one determine whether a law is *just or unjust*? A **just law** is a man made code that squares with the moral law or the law of God. An **unjust law** is a code that is out of harmony with the moral law. To put it in the terms of St. Thomas Aquinas: **An unjust law is a human law that is not rooted in eternal law and natural law. Any law that uplifts human personality is just. Any law that degrades human personality is unjust**....

> ▷ ...I submit that an individual who breaks a law that conscience tells him is unjust, and who willingly accepts the penalty of imprisonment in order to arouse the conscience of the community over its injustice, is in reality expressing the highest respect for law...

▶ **NOTE:** Please realize that this specific train of thought is strong in American society today, and

LEADERS must work to change it through positive and righteous leadership!

▶ National leaders must strongly consider using the public school system to teach ***Leadership and Positive Human Behavior Skills*** and how failing to apply key concepts may work to land a person in prison and possibly ruin their lives for good. This knowledge must be routinely taught in grades K-12 and within every college degree pattern just like the basic level sciences. *Moreover, national leaders must take steps to ensure every public school is funded at the same level where each student will receive equal mentorship and formal education.* **Only then will NO CHILD BE LEFT BEHIND...HOT!**

▶ National leaders must place emphasis on preventing criminal activity versus routinely taking the current law enforcement (reactive in nature) course of action. This can be done by considering the following recommendations:

  ▷ Taking true steps to understand ***Abraham Harold Maslow's Hierarchy of Needs*** and how Physiological needs, Security needs, Belonging needs, Self-Esteem needs, and Self-Actualization needs play into the decisions humans make that might land them in jail or prison.

  ▷ Taking steps to prevent poverty extremes where some humans are forced to live at the level of animals when they can see other people living in abundance all around them; and therefore, are motivated to take illegal steps to obtain the high life and all the fine extras that may potentially come into play!

▷ Taking steps to rebuild living environments in effort to eliminate the Criminal Justice *"Broken Windows Theory"* as devised by criminologist James Q. Wilson and George Kelling where residents of high crime areas feel America has left them behind in a dilapidated community and does not care about them, so why should they care for others (?). The true outcome is that national leaders may be perceived as criminals themselves; therefore, some local citizens may think anything goes in their minds resulting in possible harm to others! **HOT!**

▷ Taking steps to ensure police officers and loss prevention experts (i.e., Human Sheep Dogs) are formally educated in the criminal justice, security management, psychology, sociology, human relations and/or homeland security professions, and are paid where they can all maintain a descent American living. If this does not happen, some police officers (and all it takes is a few to cause negative public opinion) will become "Wolves" and prey on the citizens they are paid to protect (i.e., the Sheep)! **Why?** *Well, people are professional by trade; yet, they are human by nature!*

► National Leaders must take steps to seriously address racism, ageism, sexism, and specifically sexual or physical assault! This can easily be done via sound and honest education! Note that hate mongers have used lectures, books, and the internet (as a minimum) to solicit funds contribution by supporters and to build memberships, but what has the nation done publically and nationally via the media (written or spoken) to address hate group recruiting efforts?

► National leaders must continue to stand behind **"Free**

Speech", but we must be mature and smart about how we do it! For instance, if we continue to belittle our American police force in motion pictures and the music industry, then how or why should the average undereducated person respectfully view this authoritative position? For example, the military basically serves a similar purpose as peace officers (e.g., government law enforcement worldwide), but are portrayed by the American media in a true heroic fashion! This brings considerable pride to our armed forces that is not heavily enjoyed by our police forces. However, we do have peace officers whose performance is less than honorable, but our media seems to be so heavily focused on negative news that their actions are continuously pushed forward with limited focus on outstanding police officers. This type of news reporting backed by negative portrayals of the police in motion pictures and music can send strong signals that police officers are dishonest. The outcome is that citizens will trust no one and take law enforcement into their own hands or believe anything goes if the majority of police officers are perceived as being corrupt! This will not be good for America or its homeland security programs! Additionally, leaders must know that we cannot be irresponsible in how we communicate and conduct police activities; therefore, since Americans enjoy **"Freedom of Speech"**, we must at least ensure we positively represent the police in the media at least twice as often as we communicate negative police activities. In addition, in negative police motion pictures, perhaps directors can end movies with some type of positive moral or ethical statement that actually leads citizens in a positive direction. If not, there is a potential that the average citizen will leave the theater with an even more negative outlook of my beloved police profession. Moreover, I am still waiting to hear a positive rap or pop song about the police. Do you think we will hear such a song in this century?

▶ National leaders must realize many citizens will think the U.S. wants large prison populations to make money off free or extremely cheap labor, and especially where non-violent felony offenders are concerned. In fact, the Jan 1, 1863 Presidential Emancipation Proclamation indicates that there will be no slavery in America unless a person is duly convicted of a crime. However, in modern times many prisons are now ran by corporations and these business entrepreneurs see this as a money making opportunity instead of a true crime prevention policy. So, many criminals may refuse to ever be incarcerated thereby making their apprehensions extremely violent and dangerous to law enforcement officials. Therefore, leaders must find other ways to deal with non-violent criminals other than incarceration. Perhaps prison should actually be a last resort for non-violent criminals.

▶ National leaders who may be out of touch or disconnected from the average American's livelihood must realize the negative occurrences outlined below may certainly happen in the U.S. if true crime prevention, leadership training, and positive human behavior education is not thoroughly implemented. For instance...

  ▷ Many humans who reside in depressed low income areas may branch out and offend wealthier Americans as seen in the 2007 Washington Red Skin football player critical incident where team member Mr. Sean Taylor was attached and murdered in his own luxury home by Venjah K. Hunte and three accomplices who were all under 20 years old. It should also be noted that Mr. Hunte was from a middle class family as reported online by EncyclCentral.com, 2008.

▷ Disgruntled people (e.g., high, middle, or low class) who do not want to fairly compete for descent jobs and desired mates will join hate groups where some charismatic leader will deliver hate speeches motivated via some form of religion where members hurt innocent Americans. These charismatic leaders will continue to deliver hate speeches since they will obtain their "Belonging, Self-Esteem, and Self-Actualization Needs" from organizational members and periodically collect donated funds to pay for their "Physiological Needs" (i.e., primary spiritual motivation). Additionally, many of these members will motivate execution of a concept called **"Leaderless Resistance"** as communicated by Bruce Hoffman in his book titled "Inside Terrorism" where common citizens (or non-citizens) will conduct terrorist acts on their own accord as witnessed in the Oklahoma City Bombing by Timothy MVeigh and Terry Nichols, etc.

▷ Organized criminal organizations from all continents may continue to flourish on American soil as seen in their home nations. This will work to increase criminal activity to include human trafficking operations regardless of current legislation that bans federal employees from participation in certain off-duty activities worldwide that directly contributes to human trafficking crimes.

▷ Americans may give up on neighborhood law enforcement in effort to protect themselves and family and take crime prevention into their own hands where fair and just criminal justice system procedures will not be implemented. This can already be seen when criminal organizations conduct their own police actions to either eliminate money making competition or to police their own members.

▷ White collar crimes will continue to devastate America since potential subjects are not always seriously corrected or punished for their crimes like many street criminals. This perceived lack of unfair punishment is also witnessed by the general populace and can work to motivate criminal activity at large since citizens may portray the entire criminal justice system as playing unfairly!

▶ Finally, but definitely not the completion of this short list; citizens will give up on the government and criminal activity may get out of control as seen years ago in the **Mel Gibson** movies titled **"Mad Max or The Road Warrior."** This is happening right now in big and small cities across America! Just look around outside of high class living environments and you will see it. Of course, not on a Hollywood level or stage; yet, it is certainly present!

▷ **BOTTOM LINE:** We must take steps to enhance America now as a tribal team or we will fall just like Rome in one hundred years or less! This is something citizens who love America dearly do not want to happen. *Therefore, I stand ready to help our nation in any way I can! This book is my initial contribution!* Additionally, perhaps it might be wise to critically look at our criminal justice system and make essential improvements now just like successful corporations make fundamental changes to stay competitive and make a profit in the current market. It is obvious that no distinguished body or organization can remain effective while it stands still and the world revolves around it! It should go without saying that any organization or nation that fails to evolve will certainly become ineffective! Many citizens believe our criminal justice system has become ineffective already, but are not in any position to provide substantial positive change! Therefore, national leaders must take positive action to enhance our nation NOW!

SPECIAL NOTE: *Each checklist was created as a stand-alone guide. Therefore information contained in one checklist may be contained in another.*

CHECKLIST 31
Human Computer or Brain Enhancement Checklist

This is the last chapter of this short book for an important reason. Many leaders have made the following statement for years and it has truly stood the test of time and goes something like this, "*The mind is a terrible thing to waste.*" However, millions of people all over the planet have become victims of crimes or have become criminals themselves due in part to an improperly programmed human computer that biologist call the "Human Brain." People often do not think about it, but if a person were to purchase a top notch computer and took it home they would quickly realize that in order to make the computer function at its highest capability additional software must be purchased and installed on the computer. Well, the brain works the same way, and no psychologist or sociologist should be required to tell people this. The answer is quite simple because humans are born into this world unable to speak or walk and over time slowly gain knowledge that will allow them to effectively perform basic functions—but, this is not enough. Just like a computer requires additional software to function at its peak performance; so does the human brain, but the term software is replaced by the terms education, information, or knowledge. Moreover, the good thing is the human brain is a better product than any computer, simply because the human brain has no memory storage problems. A person can load the human brain with new information for as long as they keep their bodies in top physical condition!

Furthermore, a great deal of our human knowledge or brain software is acquired via parents, grade school, and even the streets; but this knowledge is quite limited in scope, and sometimes may even be inferior based on your actual parents or school district. Therefore, these select educational groups will not prepare you totally for a successful and safe life in America. As a matter of fact, not obtaining the appropriate level of information or education via college, technical training, military service, leadership and management courses, great parents, or mentors in effort to soundly develop effective thought processes may lead to the following human shortfalls (as a minimum).

Potential Shortfalls and Educational Mentorship Advice:

▶ Violent street gang leaders will be able to manipulate YOU (the individual) primarily because of non-existent or substandard parental mentorship or your economic standing in life; thereby, motivating you to join their criminal organization as a means to obtain survival, security, belonging, self-esteem, and self-actualization needs. The end result is that YOU (the individual) will be coerced into partaking in criminal acts that hurt others, could possibly harm you, or land you in a prison. The worst part of this scenario is creation of the societal term called, *"Black on Black Crime"* or some other similar yet cultural unique terminologies. Then the unforgivable end result is that citizens who reside in areas where *"Black on Black*

Crime" is heavy, actually reside in an environment more hostile than the past environments terrorized by what Thomas Norman identifies as *Class 5 Terrorist Organizations* which includes the Ku Klux Klan (KKK) in his book titled Risk Analysis and Security Countermeasure Selection (2010). *So, the modern question is, "Will we now have a group of people who should be called the **Black KKK**, the **Hispanic KKK**, the **Asian KKK**, or the **Native American KKK** who specifically harm people who look like them and other undesirables in which they come in contact?"*

▶ Some religious leaders will be able to play on human ignorance by telling certain groups of people that GOD/Jehovah/Allah created them and Satan created all people seen as being different than their group even if they all have a head, two arms, two eyes, a nose, a mouth, two legs, two feet, two ears, identical sex organs, a soul, and call their Earthly creator GOD and not Satan. Due to ignorance, some people who find it difficult to compete in our globalized society will look for ways to reduce their perceived competition for scarce resources by creating methods to eliminate undesirable populations. In the end, innocent people will be hurt by these humans and/or excessive amounts of potentially descent Americans will conduct crimes landing them in prison just like many gang or hate group members, and this will not be good for Homeland Security Programs. Moreover, charismatic religious leaders who call themselves Priest/Pastor will boldly take pride in taking his/her monetary donation from the audience in attendance! Yes, the Priest may actually take pride in manipulating a group of people who are less knowledgeable than themselves. For him or her, the end result is money in their pockets, house & car note paid, hot water running, and the lights powered in their home! **NOTE:** Religion(s) can be used by organizations and/or charismatic leaders to justify that some select group of humans were not created by GOD; therefore, their human eradication would be justifiable! Ignorant or evil people will buy wholeheartedly into this ideology if they stand to profit from it like many Nazi followers profited by taking resources that once belonged to incarcerated and/or murdered Jews!

► Furthermore, although I am personally a CHRISTIAN by birth assignment *(i.e., a believer in God who is also called Jehovah or Allah depending on your language)* and the Messiah *(i.e., Jesus, Yeshiva, or Yahweh depending on your language)*; I am wise enough to know that Angels did not write the Torah, the Bible, the Koran, or any other religious book. In fact, the above religious books (and others) are being translated, printed, distributed and sold by one of several book manufacturing corporations that exist all over the planet right now. They are amongst the best selling textbooks on Earth, and have earned corporations millions of dollars over the centuries, which is almost every corporation's primary goal— PROFIT! Yes, I know that a group of men once met at select locations and determined what stories should be printed in these religious books and what stories should be left out. Additionally, I once read a book that indicated the Egyptians had developed over fifty commandments they used to guide their people (search the Internet for detailed knowledge) before Moses (once an Egyptian Prince) came down a holy mountain with the Hebrew Ten Commandments; which by the way, are not that different in fabrication than many of the original Egyptian commandments. And speaking of Commandments, I honestly wish another Commandment was added, and that would be *"Thou Shall Not Be Greedy."* This Commandment alone would have probably deterred centuries of worldwide human trafficking programs (e.g., B.C. slavery and A.C. slavery); wars over land and/or natural resources; white & blue collar crime, etc and/or would have definitely helped prosperous humans think and positively react to the conditions other humans must live life under. Or perhaps these conditions would have never been allowed by leaders to take form. Finally, the New Testament talks about the large amounts of people who are going to go to heaven, but when I look around I predominately see humans who primarily care about self only. So, my question is, *"How many people are going to Hell?"* Well these numbers are not highlighted in the New Testament, but Hell is talked about quite frequently, as if used as a scare tactic to motivate Godly performance in people. This even sounds peculiar to me, being that professional leaders indicate fear cannot be used to motivate consistent favorable behavior in employees—and I know the Creator is wiser than all men! Yet, our Criminal Justice system has also failed to prevent criminal activity through the warning of imprisonment. This is simply because the average criminal does not plan on getting **CAUGHT** and going to prison, and is definitely not thinking about going to Hell. So, in closing, I must ask this question, *"Why does the Creator have to scare humans about potentially burning up in Hell for their sins, when this obviously has not even happened to Satan."* Why not just make all evil people disappear. Well, the key point to this long dissertation is that the Creator gave us all a mind; therefore, we must use it wisely by filling it with knowledge; thereby, causing it to work as best it can!

▶ We must realize that Politicians will play off human ignorance to help them maintain stellar government employment which is what American Pageant historians refer to as the *"Government Spoils System."* For instance, if the dominant populace wants minorities to hold a subordinate level in government; thereby, eliminating any competition over the good things in life, then it just might be prosperous for a Politician to join an organization like the KKK and actually legislate laws to keep a certain segment of society in its place. And by accomplishing this task, work to ensure citizens who have the same vision will definitely vote for him or her on election day. If you do your research, you will find this statement to be true, and democratic governments all over the world have members who play into the beliefs of the majority even when the dominant society is horribly wrong!

▶ Some undereducated and educated humans will also be capitalized upon within prison systems all over the world if not educated properly. It seems thousands of people do not understand that laws have been written to incarcerate large numbers of undesirable people for crimes we law enforcement professionals call "Vice Crimes", and vice crimes are typically non-violent crimes like prostitution, unsanctioned state gambling, or unsanctioned drug distribution, etc. Of course, vice crimes do not include the big three crimes (i.e., murder, child molestation, and serial rape), but the lesser crimes in which the average person generally may not receive any substantial physical loss. This is because some citizens actually look for the prostitute, illegal drug dealer, or illegal gambler just to participate in activities they believe will bring them joy instead of pain. The major problem associated with these crimes is that people convicted of vice crimes are routinely imprisoned for decades, while corporations that dump hazardous chemicals into Earth's seas or implants unnatural biological mechanisms into crops and animals that humans consume often times only receive minimal fines, and sometimes not even a fine if they successfully appeal the court verdict. Moreover, citizens must know that corporations have also become heavily involved in the prison system, where some traditional prison institutions have outsourced prison security operations to civilian corporations, and now prisoners are now incarcerated by corporations. This is somewhat beneficial for state or federal penitentiaries, since facility operations cost is substantially decreased. Yet, while incarcerated in these civilian ran prisons you (the potential prisoner) may now manufacture products sold at the Mall or shipped to factories for insertion into some electronic device, etc. Yet, the inmate will not be paid minimum wage, but may get .50

cents per hour if they are lucky. In fact, this down-sizing/outsourcing of the prison system can actually work to reduce employment by law abiding teenagers or undereducated adults who potentially might work in factories that produced corporate products sold at the Mall. So, the question is, *"What happens to the descent young American seeking employment when corporate ran prisons do not need their services to produce products because the commodities are now produced in some prison for free?"* Will they now become criminals in effort to satisfy their basic survival needs and end up in a corporate ran prison? The answer is many young and older citizens will fall into this situation if they do not wake up and recognize what I call the **American Rat Trap** is true and real (see end of Checklist 4 for more information on the subject)!

▶ Citizens must realize that many leaders will make the statement, *"The world not fair, so get used to it."* If you hear this, you must realize these people have bought totally into the system since the system has effectively taken care of their needs; and this should not come as a surprise to you, because the average citizen is really concerned about self only. However, what this negative attitude works to create is more people willing to participate in anything as long as their needs are attained; thus, possibly bringing harm to your family. This can be observed all over the world. For instance, I once read a non-fiction book written by **Hans J. Massaquoi (1999),** a Jet Magazine editor/writer who was born in Nazi Germany to a German mother and African father during the rise and fall of Hitler called **"Destined To Witness",** and Massaquoi remarked in his book that there was a hospital janitor who followed Hitler's Nazi organization because it meant that he could move up life's strata by taking place in the removal of undesirable populations (i.e., Jews and others). Well, as history records, this did happen; yet, this hospital janitor became the Hospital Administrator and immediately took steps to bring down the people who were once higher in life than he. Not only did this include firing disliked personnel, but also involved sexual harassment of nurses who probably would not have thought twice about dating him as a janitor. This author also outlined in the book that Africans kidnapped in Africa during this time frame were actually encaged in German public Zoos right along with the animals, and whenever his mother would take him to the Zoo these Africans would look at him, since they could see his African genes, as if to say, *"Kid you know this is not right—help us."* But there was definitely not much a culturally mixed child could do in Nazi Germany. He was lucky that he was part German, or else he would have been murdered by this evil cult like millions of others. The point is; people who fall into this category have accepted the norm, rather good or evil, primarily because their basic needs (and probably more) are being satisfied as long as the current government is in place. And for this German hospital janitor—his government was Nazi Germany! Failure to recognize this scheme could land people in jail or a cemetery. **NOTE TO REMEMBER:** Corporate prisons now operate in towns that would probably be "Ghost Towns" if it were not for the new community jobs. So now there is employment, and basic needs are being met; so who cares about some 16 year old poor kid caught selling small amounts of crack in New York City, and is now serving ten years in a prison located in Montana? However, corporate criminals who have dumped thousands of pounds of poisonous chemicals into rivers and oceans and are still sitting in restaurants dining on a plates that probably cost over one hundred dollars a meal. So, as said in the military, ***"Stay Alert and Stay Alive."***

▶ Furthermore, the lack of quality education; money to take care of basic survival needs; and/or desire for fame and riches may cause great entertainers to participate in movies and music videos that actually become negative training videos for young people, where they automatically assume because a big star is performing some criminal role then that must be a life expectation of them. Therefore, some young and old citizens may go into the streets and live out what is fictitiously displayed in make-believe music videos or motion pictures; thereby, helping to create a hostile living environment where the police are despised and/or people are murdered by some economic gang or hate group as seen throughout the nation and world. For example, I know many young people who saw the movie "Scar Face" and now hang posters of this fictional drug dealer on their house hold walls as if everything in this motion picture was morally and ethnically correct even though the lead character was displayed as a murderer and illegal drug dealer. Now, this is scientific, and a person need only consult with a psychologist or sociologist to be professionally informed on how media can affect young people in a positive or negative manner. Of course this should not come as a surprise to Americans, because modern media is effectively used to motivate consumers to buy products even if they do not actually need them!

▶ Finally, lack of adequate education could miss diagnose the reason for a person becoming a looser or a "Thug" as often communicated in modern times. The simple truth is this; it is easy to be a non-achiever or part of the criminal element. **All you have to do; is do absolutely nothing!** You do not have to listen to your parents, listen to honorable leaders, use quality religious books as dynamic guides in life, or even substantially participate in grade school. Yes, it easy to be a failure or criminal, but eventually you will pay dearly for not preparing yourself for quality life. In the end you may be incarcerated, crippled, or murdered by people who also choose this course of life. Yet, it is easy to be a thug, because there is no school that teaches criminal activity—one must learn on the job. **Yet, it is somewhat difficult to be a winner!** A person must go to school and learn while they are there! One must be aware of activities that will land them in the **American Rat Trap** and steer far away from them. Citizens must also associate with good people just like criminals associate with other criminals. However, the outcome will be promising even if a person does not become rich, they should be able to easily obtain their basic human survival needs and live happily. **THE BOTTOM LINE:** Please realize you must work hard for the good things in life, just like professional football players work extremely hard to win a Super Bowl. Many have worked extremely hard for decades just to get a Super Bowl opportunity, and for those who win, they will carry a ring of excellence for life and be loved by millions!

In closure, the lack of quality mentorship provided by exceptional people who care about you or the lack of formal education that provides critical information may cause people to make unwise decisions; thus; bringing potentially harmful situations into their lives! Therefore, the solution to this potential problem is to seek mentorship from any descent person you know. Additionally, you must pay attention in school and pursue formal college education as soon as you can. If you do not have the money for college, then go get a loan. It will be worth it! If the loan will not work for you, and you have managed to avoid the **American Rat Trap** and have a clean police record, then consider joining the military and have the Department of Defense pay for your education while you receive quality technical, leadership, and management training in exchange for your support to fight America's enemies. Now, many people will say this is too high of a risk just to obtain a free college education, but it is really no more dangerous than walking the streets of America in a gang and/or not in a gang. Few people know it, but the FBI keeps annual statistics on murders in America, and over 13,600 people were murdered in the US in 2009 (an average amount per year). Now, please take note that there are many other people murdered in the US not included in this count because their bodies have not been discovered, but you should know the **Middle Eastern War** has been going on since 2003 and unfortunately 6,000 American military members have lost their lives. Yet, if 13,000-15,000 people are normally murdered in America in a given year, then how many people were shot and did not die? I am certain that this number is well over 30,000 per year, and then you can add the accidental deaths to the list (e.g., vehicle accidents, work center accidents, aircraft accidents, surgical accidents, train accidents, etc.) and multiply the final number by eight (i.e., eight plus year Middle Eastern War); thereby, putting stateside American loss of life via violent crime **substantially higher** than American military member deaths in Iraq and Afghanistan combined. The bottom line is that if you go off statistics, it is safer to bring peace to Iraq and Afghanistan (and other nations in the world) than it is to walk down a given street in America—and especially as a gang member/criminal! And guess what, while taking part in Iraqi battles that actually do not occur every day, one can enroll in free college courses when safe behind garrison protected walls. Moreover, there are also military education programs, where military personnel can contribute relatively small amounts of money in exchange for thousands of dollars in educational assistance funds **(e.g., Post 9/11 GI Bill)** that can be utilized either on or off active duty! Yet, you will not have to use these saved funds, because there is a military program called ***Tuition Assistance*** that may pay up to 100% of college class cost. Now, some people will not join the military for educational purposes, but many may, and will be thankful for this great American military benefit, plus many others!

So, there you have it. Please educate and then elevate, and do not be blinded by evil acts just because your personal life may be heavenly, or commit criminal acts because it is blindly assume that one will not be CAUGHT and prosecuted. You must remember, *"All criminals will eventually pay for their horrendous crimes!"* Somehow, this seems to be the Creator's way of doing business (i.e.., Karma, What Goes Around, Comes Around concept, or the Universal Law of Attraction).

Always keep your eyes wide open, because we should be nurturing and protecting all humans, and protecting our Earth so future generations can happily reside on this paradise planet our Creator (or nature) made for us! If people actually listen, then perhaps one day HUMANS will realize that we are from the same Earthly tribe, and hate, crime, and WAR will cease to exist! But in the mean time, please educate and elevate yourself! Additionally, please think long and hard about these slogans:

► We cannot triumph over evil if good people do absolutely nothing! Therefore, democratic populations must wake up and understand they have strength in numbers. This is ultra important when it comes down to electing a descent, strong, wise, fair, and caring leader into any nation's presidential office!

► Realize many good people honestly called "**SHEEP DOGS**" (i.e., human population protectors) that are hired to protect the "**SHEEP**" (i.e., human population) from the "**WOLVES**" (i.e., hate mongers and criminals) have a major shortfall to eliminate. And the shortfall is that there are millions of **WOLVES** who are camouflaged as **SHEEP** and **SHEEP DOGS**; thereby, hurting **SHEEP DOG** efforts to effectively and honorably protect of **SHEEP**. We must be on the lookout for **WOLVES**, and legally remove them from leadership positions when they are uncovered. Just like it is written our Creator (i.e., God/Jehovah/Allah) did to one of his/her/its most famous and beautiful fallen Angels named Satan (i.e., the Devil or Lucifer).

▶ **NOTE:** If elected, leaders with predominately **SHEEP** leadership characteristics must not become complacent and think/wish things are GOOD when they are NOT; thus developing laws or rules that make other **SHEEP** feel good, but actually benefit the **WOLVES**! In fact, in our world a **national LEADER** must never be a **SHEEP** but always a **SHEEP DOG** (i.e., Protection of the Flock)!

> ▷ **Arab Parable:** *An army of sheep **led by a lion** would defeat an army of lions **led by a sheep***.

▶ *It's a hard knock life for us—we get tricked and kicked* (American Hip Hop artist—Jay Z)! Such will be the life for those who do not realize all forms of advanced education is important and refuse to take action to obtain it. These people will be capitalized upon by other better connected and educated humans for centuries, which may surely bring unwanted pain and suffering upon them. A great closing example is the prostitution business. This system is managed by a person who calls themselves a "Pimp" or "Madam" and receives cash payment from people (i.e., prostitutes) who have sexual relations with others for a monetary fee. Now, a wise person will immediately wonder why a person who has a product to sale, would sale that product and then give the profit to a person who does no real work. Yet, undereducated people are still manipulated by Pimps and Madams, and the end result is that the prostitute can be imprisoned, assaulted, murdered, or even contract some incurable sexual transmitted disease while the Pimp or Madam financially benefits. *Now, a wiser person might clearly analyze the prostitution business for what it is and realize the "Prostitute" is the actual money maker (i.e., CEO), and if any male or female is employed in their business, they would normally be employed as an Escort Service Manager or in a true Security Role (only), just like many wealthy people detail and pay personal security guards.*

Yes, being **ignorant** is extremely dangerous—since it is dangerous to SELF and all others that come in contact with an ignorant person. It is often a hard knock life for many, since these people often get tricked and kicked!

FINAL NOTE: Wise humans might seriously consider reading **Proverbs** found in the Old Testament. It will provide great guidance on living life in this world. Many people do not know it, but there are **31 Proverbs**—one for each day, and **Proverbs 31** even tells you what your ideal mate should be like! **In my personal opinion, PROVERBS is the BEST chapter in the entire Bible.** It will definitely give you guidance to protect yourself, your family, and your soul! And guess what, **"This knowledge has truly withstood the test of time!"**

"*Our identity, our essence—in sum, who we are—becomes apparent by virtue of the entire presentation we make when we are interacting with others.*"

Nelson Fabian

SPECIAL NOTE: *Each checklist was created as a stand-alone guide. Therefore information contained in one checklist may be contained in another.*

CHECKLIST 32
References

► Adams, T. (1992).*Harden the target.* Griffin Publishing Company

► Air Force Times (2012). *Colonel's wife accused of killing mistress.* A Garnet Company

► Barack Obama, B. (2006). *The audacity of hope.* Crown Publishers

► Bennet, L. (2003).*Before the mayflower.* Johnson Publishing Company

► Crowe, T. (2000).*Crime prevention through environment design.* 2nd Edition. Butterworth Heinemann

► Fabian, N. (2001). *The importance of writing well.* Journal of Environment Health.

► Hoffman, B. (1998). *Inside terrorism.* Columbia University Press

► Jane's. (1999). *World insurgency and terrorism.* Jane's Information Group Limited, Sentinel House, UK

► JET Magazine. (1999). *ACLU tells what you should do if stopped by police.* Vol. 95, NO. 23. Johnson Publishing Company

► Massaquoi, H. (1999). *Destined to witness. Growing up black in Nazi Germany.* William Morrow and Company INC, NY.

► Loewen J. (1995). *Lies my teacher told me.* The New Press

▶ Norman, T. (2010). *Risk analysis and security counter-measure selection*. CRC Press

▶ Pierce, W. (1978). *The turner diaries*. National Vanguard Books

▶ Purpura, P. (2002). *Security and loss prevention*, Butterworth-Heinemann

▶ Robinson, R. (1999). *Issues in security management. Thinking critically about security*. Butterworth & Heinemann

▶ Rock, C. (2000-2005). *The chris rock show*. HBO

▶ Stars and Stripes. (2006-2007). *Iraq Articles*. Stars and Stripes

▶ USA Today. (Jul 1999). Across the USA reports. USA Today

▶ United States Air Force. (1990). *Bomb threat aid*. Air Force Form 440.Department of the AF

▶ Zinn, H. (2003).*The people's history of the united states*.1942 to present. The New Press

CHECKLIST 33
Acknowledgements

The authorship of this book would not have been possible if it were not for several outstanding mentors and professional organizations that helped develop my protection and communication skills. For instance, it was the United States Air Force's (USAF) brilliant ROTC program executed at E.E. Smith Senior High, Fayetteville, North Carolina that motivated me to join the USAF to become a Security Policeman in 1981. In this profession, I was instructed on security management, law enforcement, information and personnel security, leadership, management, mentorship, and followership skills to include tutorship on how to become a stellar human and **SHEEP DOG** (i.e., Protector of the human flock of **SHEEP** from the **WOLVES**). Yes, the USAF, and later the Defense Threat Reduction Agency (DTRA) invested thousands of dollars in making me a competent protector of people and critical war fighting resource; however, they were not my only teachers.

I would also like to give credit to my parents **Arnetta White** and **Henry White** who sent me to church as a child to learn right versus wrong from great traditional Southern Baptist Ministers. It was these beloved people who helped me determine what direction in life I should follow in effort to eliminate as much **negativity** from my life as possible.

Additionally, I would like to thank my lovely wife **La Gulia Toomes White** for her support who in my humble opinion is as close as a person comes to being an Angel in human form. She stood by me during long hours at the job and military deployments to austere locations all over the world, and she did this while being a superb and supportive wife and mother. I could not have asked for a better spouse; yet, I must admit, this was a professional matter of choice, as was her decision to marry me!

Furthermore, I would like to pay tribute to my 14-year old son **Malik Omar White** and my 10-year old daughter **Iyanna Oman White** that built their protection-oriented skills by aiding in review of this book and providing dynamic input. I would also like to thank my 7-year old son **Kwali Ome White** who could be counted on to assist in any required administrative task.

Moreover, I would like to thank **AuthoHouse** for being a great organization and helping me publish this self-authored book designed to help others—i.e., those humans who wish to live in peace and enjoy life in America and all other places throughout the world.

In closing, I would like to thank our Creator for making me whole and giving me the guidance to become a descent American, **SHEEP DOG** (i.e., Protector), LEADER, and fellowman of all humans who inhabit the Earth!

SPECIAL NOTE: Special acknowledgement goes out to the family members and friends who provided either concurrence and/or expert feedback into the development of this document:

► Bobby Hamilton (former Air Force Security Policeman)

- Charles McDonald (former Air Force Civil Engineer)

- Christopher Tate (former Air Force Security Policeman)

- Herman Johnson (former Air Force Security Policeman)

- James Calhoun (former Army Soldier)

- Jeff Jones (former Air Force Security Policeman)

- Maurice Washington (former Air Force Security Policeman and Los Angeles Police Department Officer)

- Phyllis A. Barnette (Teacher – One of Virginia's Finest)

- Reginald Diamond (former AF Security Policeman & California Corrections Officer)

- Richard Spence (USAF SMSgt/First Sergeant & US Post Master)

- Timothy Sinclair (former Army Soldier)

- Yonsenia White (former Professor, Virginia Tech)
    * I retain all copyrights.

YOUR BROTHERS KEEPER
SHEEP DOG
(Human Flock Protector)

Mr. Kevin Andre White
(*American Society for Industrial Security,*
Certified Protection Professional #14280)
KEEP YOUR FAMILY SAFE VIA
PROPER EDUCATION

PRESIDENTAL QUOTE:
"Pull the string, and it will follow wherever
you wish. Push it, it will go nowhere at all."
                    Dwight D. Eisenhower

AUTHOR
KEVIN A. WHITE, CMSGT, USAF
Retired September 1, 2011
(30 years active duty service)

TRUE QUOTE:
"An army of sheep led by a lion would defeat an army of lions led by a sheep."

Arab Proverb